Rethinking Performance Measurement

Performance measurement remains a vexing problem for business firms and other kinds of organizations. This book explains why: the performance we want to measure (long-term cash flows, long-term viability) and the performance we can measure (current cash flows, customer satisfaction, etc.) are not the same. The "balanced scorecard," which has been widely adopted by US firms, does not solve these underlying problems of performance measurement and may exacerbate them because it provides no guidance on how to combine dissimilar measures into an overall appraisal of performance. A measurement technique called activity-based profitability analysis (ABPA) is suggested as a partial solution, especially to the problem of combining dissimilar measures. ABPA estimates the revenue consequences of each activity performed for the customer, allowing firms to compare revenues with costs for these activities and hence to discriminate between activities that are ultimately profitable and those that are not.

MARSHALL W. MEYER is Richard A. Sapp Professor and Professor of Management and Sociology at The Wharton School of the University of Pennsylvania.

Rethinking
Performance
Measurement

Beyond the Balanced Scorecard

MARSHALL W. MEYER
The Wharton School, University of Pennsylvania

CAMBRIDGE
UNIVERSITY PRESS

PUBLISHED BY THE PRESS SYNDICATE OF THE UNIVERSITY OF CAMBRIDGE
The Pitt Building, Trumpington Street, Cambridge CB2 1RP, United Kingdom

CAMBRIDGE UNIVERSITY PRESS
The Edinburgh Building, Cambridge, CB2 2RU, UK
40 West 20th Street, New York, NY 10011-4211, USA
477 Williamstown Road, Port Melbourne, VIC 3207, Australia
Ruiz de Alarcón 13, 28014 Madrid, Spain
Dock House, The Waterfront, Cape Town 8001, South Africa

http://www.cambridge.org

First published 2002

Printed in the United Kingdom at the University Press, Cambridge

Typeface Sabon 10/13 pt   *System* LATEX 2$_\varepsilon$ [TB]

A catalogue record for this book is available from the British Library

ISBN 0 521 81243 7 hardback

Contents

Figures

Tables

Preface

Performance measurement is in an uproar. The collapse of the internet bubble, the bankruptcy of Enron, and the erosion of confidence in the accounting profession have placed the problem of measuring the performance of the firm – and of other kinds of organizations – squarely in the public arena. Enron's bankruptcy, in particular, is a watershed event. On the surface, it raises the issue of how a firm reporting pretax profits of $1.5 billion from the third quarter of 2000 through the third quarter of 2001 could file for bankruptcy the next quarter. The answers proffered so far are the expected: sharp if not fraudulent financial practices, cozy relationships with auditors and their consulting arms, even cozier relationships with Wall Street analysts, and directors so dazzled by Enron's growth and generous directors' fees that they failed to exercise proper fiduciary responsibility.

But there remains an underlying problem so daunting that to raise it is almost heretical: can we accurately measure the performance of firms like Enron or, for that matter, any firm? I raise this question because the answer is not clear. For decades we have accepted that the performance of non-profit organizations like hospitals and universities is difficult to gauge. To be sure, performance measures for hospitals and universities abound (mortality/morbidity/acceptance/graduation rates, patient/student satisfaction, professional reputation), but most are unsatisfactory because they are incomplete or susceptible to deliberate distortion or both.

Until recently, firms have been privileged because we have assumed that the profit motive simplifies the measurements of their performance. Perhaps it once did. But no longer. As the internet bubble, Enron, and the travail of the accounting profession have shown, metrics (e.g. pro forma earnings) and accounting practices (e.g. off-balance-sheet assets) now commonplace have obscured the performance of firms. But for managers simplicity has long since vanished. The appearance of the balanced scorecard ten years ago signaled how complicated – and uncertain – performance measurement has become. The balanced scorecard was intended to make sense of the myriad of financial and non-financial performance measures that emerged in the 1980s and early 1990s by organizing them into four broad categories. But the scorecard has floundered as a device for measuring and rewarding performance. This book shows why (see chapter 3). Nevertheless, the scorecard has remained immensely popular as a tool for tracking progress toward strategic objectives, an aspiration far more modest than measuring and rewarding the performance of the firm and its people.

Why has performance measurement proved so challenging? Part of the answer lies in the gap between what we want to measure and what we can measure. We want to measure (or predict, if we cannot measure) how people and firms will perform. But we can only measure how people and firms have performed in the past. And the past is not necessarily a reliable guide to the future. Part of the answer lies in human nature: people will exploit the gap between what we want to measure and what we can measure by delivering exactly what is measured rather than the performance that is sought but cannot be measured. Part of the answer lies in the complexity of organizations we have created: the more complicated the organization, the more performance measures are taken and the more dissimilar those measures are – hence the more difficult it is to understand the actual performance of the organization. (It is likely that Enron's managers understood this principle better than their auditors.)

The gap between what we want to measure and what we can measure is endemic. The gap will not go away unless, of course, we revert to a command economy and quotas – the hallmarks of the failed experiment called socialism. Human nature will not change, but we can monitor measures and replace measures no longer discriminating good performance from bad because people have learned too well how to deliver what is measured rather than what is sought. Organizational complexity will not go away either. But we can analytically simplify otherwise complex organizations and reduce, if not eliminate, the dissimilarity of measures.

What I call ABPA – activity-based profitability analysis – is intended to accomplish this simplification by addressing some basic questions: what does the firm do for each of its customers, what does it cost, and what will customers pay for it? ABPA, to be sure, is not an all-purpose performance measurement tool. ABPA is not a panacea for all the underlying problems of performance measurement. Neither is the balanced scorecard, as will be amply demonstrated. However, ABPA, unlike the scorecard, has the virtue of focusing attention on the basics: what are we doing, what does it cost, and what will the customer pay for it? My hypothesis is that firms that persistently ask these questions will do better than firms that don't. ABPA is simply a structure for asking these questions in a disciplined way.

This project began from a persistent observation: the most common measures of organizational performance are statistically uncorrelated (see chapter 2). There are two ways to interpret this. One interpretation is that organizational performance lacks construct validity, in other words, that organizational performance does not exist. More than a few of my colleagues have taken this position, and many have had successful academic careers. Another interpretation is that sloppy thinking pervades performance measurement. This occurs because we have confused performance measures with performance. It is easy to measure something and call it performance (and then to rate and rank firms on the measure and publicize the ranking so that the measure becomes performance in people's minds). It is far more difficult to answer the fundamental questions, first, what is performance – that is, organizational performance – and, second, how to measure it. It turns out that organizational performance is not in the dictionary, which may be surprising because theatrical performance, mechanical performance, and psychological performance all are. It also turns out that theatrical performance, mechanical performance, and psychological performance, which are observable, are much easier to measure than organizational performance, which is not. The skeptic may argue that the performance of a firm is captured in its earnings and share prices. My answer is that earnings and share prices capture performance partially but far from completely. Consider the internet bubble. Consider Enron.

I owe a substantial debt to Professor Robert K. Merton. In the early stages of this research Merton persistently asked whether I was confusing performance measures with performance, in other words, had I fallen into the trap similar to operationalism, a doctrine of the 1930s asserting that the physical sciences should deal only with observables? It took me six months to understand Merton's question and much longer even to begin to answer it, and I am still not sure that I have done so satisfactorily. I am also indebted to Beth Bechky, Chris Ittner, Dave Larcker, Ian MacMillan, and Sarah Mavrinac for comments on the manuscript. Mavrinac treated the manuscript like a draft of a PhD dissertation – there were handwritten comments on practically every page. Chris Harrison of Cambridge University Press is responsible, among other things, for the title of the book. Chris is one of the smartest editors I have ever encountered. My work on performance measurement would not have been possible without the backing of several organizations, including the Reginald H. Jones Center of the University of Pennsylvania, the Russell Sage Foundation, where I was a visiting scholar for the 1993–94 academic year, and the Citibank Behavioral Sciences Research Council, which funded the research on the balanced scorecard. My deepest thanks go to all those who supported this project and to Judy, Josh, and Gabe who smiled whenever they asked, "Where's the book?"

Introduction

D ISSATISFACTION with performance measurement systems runs high. Many firms, perhaps the majority, suspect that they haven't got it right. A 1995 article in *Chief Financial Officer* begins, "According to a recent survey, 80 percent of large American companies want to change their performance measurement systems..."[1] Unsurprisingly, the turmoil in performance measurement is ongoing. Startup companies struggling for capital must continually adjust their metrics.[2] And it is commonplace for large firms to undertake annual overhauls of their performance measurement systems.[3]

Why the turmoil and dissatisfaction? One cause is the ongoing search for non-financial predictors of financial performance: "Yesterday's accounting results say nothing about the factors that actually help grow market share and profits – things like customer service innovation, R&D effectiveness, the percent of first-time quality, and employee development."[4] Another cause, ironically, is a surfeit of measures: many corporate controllers cite the burdens imposed by "newfangled performance measures" as a key source of burnout.[5] Anecdotal reports such as these suggest that executives are seeking measures that controllers and chief financial officers have so far been reluctant or unable to deliver. The result is frustration on both sides.

Whether the problem is too few or too many measures, many accountants believe that corporate performance measurement systems do not support management objectives well. According to the Institute of Management Accountants, the proportion of accountants rating their performance measures as "poor" or "less than adequate," the bottom two categories on a six-point scale where the fourth category is "adequate," has remained substantial, ranging from 35 percent in 1992 to 43 percent in 1993, 38 percent in 1995, 43 percent in 1996, 34 percent in 1997, 40 percent in 2000, and 33 percent in 2001.[6] The year-to-year changes are small and do not reveal a trend, but these IMA surveys suggest that while performance measures are changing rapidly, management accountants do not experience these changes as improvements.

Avoiding bedrock issues: the "balanced scorecard"

Firms and non-business organizations alike can no longer afford to avoid bedrock issues of performance measurement. Let's be frank. For the last decade, discussion of performance measurement has been dominated by the "balanced scorecard." Many books, articles, and cases about the balanced scorecard have appeared during that period, the *Harvard Business Review* has called the balanced scorecard one of the most important management ideas in the last seventy-five years, and an organization called the Balanced Scorecard Collaborative serves as a central clearing house for what it calls the "balanced scorecard movement."[7] What is missing from the spin surrounding the balanced scorecard is a simple fact about performance measures, the significance of which is not widely appreciated: common-sense measures used to gauge the performance of a firm are generally uncorrelated. In other words, look across a large number of firms or their business units and you will find that profitability, market share, customer satisfaction, and operating efficiency are weakly and sometimes negatively correlated. These measures move in different directions about as often as they move in tandem. Social scientists have known this for years and have drawn two conclusions. First, measuring performance is difficult (since it is not clear that performance is a single construct). Second, the choice of performance measures is often arbitrary (since it is difficult to prove that any one measure is better than others). Though neither of these conclusions is particularly useful, they would not surprise managers.

Beginning in 1992, Robert Kaplan and David Norton transformed the persistent observation that measures are generally uncorrelated into a prescription for business practice: just as pilots track multiple instruments to gauge the performance of an aircraft, managers should track multiple measures to gauge the performance of their firms. "Managers want a balanced presentation of both financial and operational measures... The scorecard brings together, in a single management report, many of the seemingly disparate elements of a company's competitive agenda..."[8] Not only is the analogy between cockpit instruments and the measures needed to guide firms compelling, but its logic is also impeccable. Consider the counterfactual. Ask whether multiple measures would be necessary if measures were strongly correlated, that is if the most common performance measures rose and fell together. The answer is this: if performance measures were strongly correlated, then all would contain essentially the same information, any one of them would contain complete information about the performance of the firm, and there would be no need for multiple measures or a "balanced scorecard."[9] For example, if customer satisfaction and bottom-line results were strongly correlated, there would be no need, except for comfort, to measure customer satisfaction since bottom-line results would signal the level of customer satisfaction. Now consider the actual. Again, performance measures are weakly correlated. Each contains different information about the performance of the firm, and scorecards utilizing multiple measures are needed to capture the performance of the firm completely. In other words, customer satisfaction (and operational performance, innovation, and so on) must be measured alongside financial results *because they are different.*

Unfortunately, the logic lying behind the scorecard approach to performance measurement can go awry when measures are put to use. While there are good reasons to measure multiple dimensions of performance, there are also strong pressures to appraise performance along one dimension: better or worse. These pressures are strongest when compensating and rewarding people's performance, but they are also present when making investment decisions. Whenever managers ask whether firm A performs better than B, whether division C performs better than D, or, most poignantly, if employee E is a better performer and hence should be compensated more generously than F, G, and H, they are tacitly if not explicitly trying to reduce performance to a single dimension.

Even Kaplan and Norton recognize these limitations of the "balanced scorecard" and are reluctant to recommend scorecards to appraise and compensate performance. Consider the following:

Norton:...firms often hesitate to link the scorecard to compensation. Kaplan: They should hesitate, because they have to be sure they have the right measures [on the scorecard]. They want to run with the measures for several months, even up to a year, before saying they have confidence in them. Second, they may want to be sure of the hardness of the data, particularly since some of the balanced scorecard measures are more subjective. Compensation is such a powerful lever that you have to be pretty confident that you have the right measures and have good data for the measures [before making the link].[10]

Note that Kaplan and Norton construe the compensation problem narrowly, as a problem of finding the "right measures." The compensation problem, in fact, is much broader. It exposes the tension between measuring performance along several dimensions and appraising performance ultimately on one dimension. Remember: scorecard measures are necessarily different. If they weren't, then they would be redundant and there would be no need for the balanced scorecard because any one measure would do. The compensation problem, moreover, raises the question of whether the "right measures" can in fact be found. "Right measures," to be sure, can be found in static environments where the parameters of performance are well understood. Go back to the cockpit analogy. Pilots know how an aircraft must perform in order to complete its mission and rely on their instruments to compare actual to required performance. In competitive environments, however, the performance required to produce a satisfactory return can change unpredictably; in other words, measures that were right can be rendered obsolete or pernicious overnight.

Rather than tackling these bedrock problems of performance measurement, Kaplan and Norton have recast the "balanced scorecard" as a management system intended to communicate strategies and objectives more effectively than non-scorecard systems: "Measurement creates focus for the future. The measures chosen by managers communicate important messages to all organizational units and employees...the Balanced Scorecard concept evolved from a performance measurement system to become the organizing framework, the operating system, for a new strategic management system."[11] I am skeptical about basing strategy on performance measures. I worry about unintended consequences, especially unintended consequences of imperfect measures – as will be shown, all performance measures are imperfect. In particular, I worry about measurement systems becoming arteriosclerotic, turning into the rigid quota systems that ruined socialist economies. "What you measure is what you get" captures the problem: if you cannot measure what you want, then you will not get what you want.

I'm not saying that we can do without performance measures, but I am saying that we should tackle bedrock issues before basing strategies on such measures. Again, the specter of quotas haunts me. I think that we should approach the bedrock issues realistically. We should assume that measuring performance is difficult. If performance measurement weren't difficult, then it wouldn't be the chronic problem that it is. I also think we should assume that performance measurement is difficult for good reasons. The good reasons, I suspect, lie in both the nature of organizations and the people in them.

Consider organizations first. The dilemma created by organizations is illustrated by Adam Smith's pin-making factory, where every worker is like an independent business – one cuts wire, a second sharpens the wire, a third solders pin heads onto the sharpened wire, a fourth boxes pins, and so forth – engaging in cash transactions with co-workers. There is no performance measurement problem because each worker has his or her own revenues and costs. There is an efficiency problem, however, since intermediate inventories will accumulate if workers fail to coordinate their efforts and produce at different rates – if the wire cutter works faster than the sharpener, for example. The solution to the efficiency problem is placing the workers under a common supervisor charged with coordinating the process; in other words, creating an organization. But solving the efficiency problem creates a performance measurement problem. There is no simple way to measure separately the contributions of the wire cutter, the wire sharpener, the solderer, and the boxer to the performance of the organization that has been created because one revenue stream has replaced the independent revenue streams that formerly existed.

Now consider the people problem. People will assume performance measures to be consequential and will strive to improve measured performance even if the performance that is measured is not the performance that is actually sought – teaching to test is illustrative. Performance measures, as a consequence, get progressively worse with use, and managers face the challenge of searching out newer and better measures – better, that is, until they deteriorate – while retaining the semblance of clarity and consistency of direction. That organizations and the people in them create impediments to measuring performance as well as we would like is central to the rethinking of performance measurement I shall propose.

The message and metaphor of the balanced scorecard were, of course, important first steps in getting at bedrock issues of performance measurement. The notion that a tool as complicated as a baseball scorecard might be needed to gauge corporate performance has jarred managers into realizing there is more to performance than the bottom line. But the message and the metaphor are now ten years old. It is time to rethink performance measurement once more.

Ideal performance measurement

The rethinking of performance measurement begins with a simple question: what properties do we look for in performance measures? Ideally, the performance measures of choice would meet the following requirements:

- Parsimony. There would be relatively few measures to keep track of, perhaps as few as three financial measures and three non-financial measures. (I have chosen three plus three arbitrarily, but I think these numbers are realistic.) Cognitive limits would be exceeded and information would actually be lost were there many more measures.
- Predictive ability. The non-financial measures would predict subsequent financial performance, in other words, the non-financials would serve as leading performance indicators and the financials as lagging indicators, as measures summarizing performance after it occurred. Non-financial measures not demonstrated to be leading indicators would be discarded unless, of course, they were tracked as matters of regulation, ethics, and security – "must-dos" for firms.
- Pervasiveness. These measures would pervade the organization – the same measures would apply everywhere. Measures pervading the organization have three key advantages over highly specific measures: they can be summed from the bottom to the top of the organization, which allows people to see connections between their results and the results of the firm; they can be decomposed downward, which gives senior managers drill-down capability; and they can be compared horizontally across different units, which facilitates improvement and performance appraisal.
- Stability. The measurement system would be stable. Measures would change gradually so as to maintain people's awareness of long-term goals and consistency in their behavior.
- Applicability to compensation. People would be compensated for performance on these measures, that is for financial results and results of non-financial measures known to be leading indicators of financial results.

The requirements of ideal performance measurement are very stringent, far more stringent than the requirements of the balanced scorecard. The balanced scorecard imposes only the two requirements on measures, parsimony and predictive ability: in principle, scorecard measures are more parsimonious than the potpourri of measures tracked by most large firms, and non-financial scorecard measures predict financial results. The scorecard does not address pervasiveness other than acknowledging that scorecards and scorecard measures are likely to vary across different parts of the organization. Nor does the scorecard address the stability of measures. Moreover, as noted, Kaplan and Norton are cautious about using scorecard measures to compensate people – for good reason, as will be seen below.

Rarely if ever do we find performance measures meeting these common-sense requirements. Here is why:

- Firms are swamped with measures, and the problem of too many measures is, if anything, getting worse, the balanced scorecard withstanding. It is commonplace for firms to have fifty to sixty top-level measures, both financial and non-financial. One of the longest lists of top-level measures I have seen includes twenty financial measures, twenty-two customer measures, sixteen measures of internal process, nineteen measures of renewal and development, and thirteen human resources measures.[12] Many firms, I am sure, have even more top-level measures.
- Our ability to create and disseminate measures has outpaced, at least for now, our ability to separate the few non-financial measures containing information about future financial performance from the many that do not. To be sure, research studies show that a myriad of non-financial measures such as customer and employee satisfaction affect financial performance, but their impact is modest, often firm- and industry-specific, and discoverable only after the fact.
- Few non-financial measures pervade the organization. It is easier to find financial measures that pervade the organization, but keep in mind that many firms have struggled unsuccessfully to drive measures of shareholder value from the top to the bottom of the organization.
- Performance measures, non-financial measures especially, never stand still. With use they lose variance, sometimes rapidly, and hence the capacity to discriminate good from bad performance. This is the use-it-and-lose-it principle in performance measurement. Managers respond by continually shuffling measures.

- Compensating people for performance on multiple measures is extremely difficult. Paying people on a single measure creates enough dysfunctions. Paying them on many measures creates more. The problem is combining dissimilar measures into an overall evaluation of performance and hence compensation. If measures are combined formulaically, people will game the formula. If measures are combined subjectively, people will not understand the connection between measured performance and their compensation.

There is a still more fundamental reason for the gap between ideal performance measurement and performance measurement as it is. The modern conception of performance, which is the economic conception of performance, renders the performance of the firm not entirely measurable. The modern conception of performance is future cash flows – "cash flows still to come"[13] – discounted to present value. In other words, we think of the firm as assets capable of generating current and future cash flows.[14] Future cash flows, by definition, cannot be measured. Nor can we measure the long-term viability and efficiency of the firm in the absence of which cash flows will dwindle or vanish. What we can and do measure are current cash flows (financial performance), potential predictors of future cash flows (non-financial measures), and proxies for future cash flows (share prices). All of these are imperfect. They are, at best, second-best measures. Note the paradox that is at the heart of efforts to improve performance measurement: knowing that most measures are second best compels us to search for better measures that are inevitably second best. If we had a different conception of performance – for example if we believed a firm's performance was its current assets rather than future cash flows – then measuring the performance of the firm would be no more complicated than measuring the performance of an airplane. One point deserves emphasis: I'm not saying that everyone subscribes to the notion of economic performance, of performance as future cash flows or even as the long-term viability and efficiency of the firm. Managers, in particular, think of performance as meeting the targets they have been assigned. I *am* saying, however, that our unease with most of the performance measures we have is due to the gap between what we can measure – current financial and non-financial results – and the future cash flows we would measure if we could.

The performance chain

To search intelligently for better, albeit second-best, performance measures, we may have to rethink the firm and the relevant units for measuring performance. Right now, we think of firms as black boxes: investment flows into the firm, activities take place, products are made and sold to customers as a result of these activities, and an income statement, balance sheet, and market valuation of the firm follow. Since financial results – the income statement, balance sheet, and market valuation – accrue to the firm as a whole or, internally, to large chunks of the firm called business units, we look for drivers of financial performance, that is non-financial measures describing internal processes, products, and customers, at the level of the entire firm or its business units. The problem with the black-box approach to the firm and performance measurement is that it masks differences within firms and their business units: so many processes take place, so many products are produced, and so many customers are served that firm- or business unit-level performance measures – which I'll call aggregate measures – conceal important sources of variation. The things a firm does well are lumped together with the things it does poorly, making it difficult to know, for example, precisely where to invest and where to cut costs. Importantly, the larger the firm and its business units, the more information about performance is obscured by aggregate performance measures.[15]

The rethinking of the firm and of the relevant units for measuring performance begins by asking where the performance of the firm comes from. The performance of the firm originates in what the firm does, in its activities or routines. These activities give rise to costs, but they also generate revenues in excess of costs to the extent that the firm's products and services add value for customers. These cash flows and the expectation of future cash flows in turn give rise to the valuation of the firm in capital markets. The causal chain running from activities to costs to revenues to the valuation of the firm in capital markets is shown in figure I.1. This 'performance chain' is an extension of Michael Porter's idea of the value chain that incorporates costs.[16]

The performance chain carries some immediate implications for performance measurement. First, the units in the performance chain bear little resemblance to the units on a typical organization chart. There are three principal units: the firm, the customer, and the activity. By

Figure I.1 The performance chain of the firm.

contrast, the units displayed on an organization chart are typically the firm, business units, functional units, and work groups within business and functional units. Many activities take place within business units, functional units, and work groups, and many customers are served, directly or indirectly, by each of them. The performance chain thus raises two questions: should firms be partitioned into units, such as activities, that are much smaller than the units shown on organization charts, and how should performance be measured on these smaller units?

Second, the performance chain shows that activities incur costs and customers supply revenues – and that revenues and costs are usually joined at the level of the firm. This raises the question of whether costs can be assigned to customers and, correspondingly, whether revenues can be assigned to activities so that revenues and costs can be compared for individual customers and activities. It is not uncommon for firms to assign costs to customers and then compare revenues to costs customer by customer. This is sometimes called customer profitability analysis. I will show below that once you assign costs to customers, you can also assign revenues to activities, in other words, you also can also compare revenues to costs activity by activity. I call this activity-based profitability analysis or ABPA. The possibility of assigning revenues and costs to individual customers and activities is one of several reasons why it may be better for performance measures to follow the performance chain than to follow the organization chart – while you can always assign costs to the units shown on an organization chart, you cannot easily assign revenues to units smaller than your profit centers or strategic business units.

The elemental conception of the firm

The performance chain also carries implications for how we think about the firm itself. Put aside your preconceptions about organizations and imagine the firm as a bundle of activities, nothing more.

These activities incur costs. These activities may also add value for customers, although they may not. When activities add value for customers, customers supply revenues to the firm. When activities do not add value, customers hold on to their wallets. The elements of the firm, then, are activities, costs, customers (who decide which activities add value and which do not), and revenues. Under the elemental conception, attention is shifted from the performance of the firm as a whole to the activities performed by the firm and the revenues and costs associated with these activities. The problem for the firm is finding those activities that add value for the customer and generate revenues in excess of costs, extending those activities, and reducing or eliminating activities that incur costs in excess of revenues. Finding the right measures of that performance becomes less of an issue, although, as we shall see, actually measuring the costs and revenues associated with activities is not always easy. Importantly, the problem of balancing or combining dissimilar measures, which is a major limitation of the balanced scorecard, disappears.

The elemental conception of the firm is a radical departure from established precepts of organizational design, but it may be time to rethink these precepts. The range of organizational designs suggested by academics and consultants is staggering. These designs include simple hierarchy, functional organization, divisional organization, matrix organization combining functional and divisional designs, circular organization, hybrid organization that is part hierarchy and part market, and network organization where lateral ties take precedence over vertical ties. All of these organizational designs fix attention on the internal architecture of the firm. What they overlook is the fact that internal architecture has receded in significance as external relationships have drawn an increasing share of managers' attention. This has occurred for several reasons: there are many more firms than ever; firms, on average, have grown somewhat smaller; firms have many more alliance and joint venture partners than they once did; managers depend increasingly on information originating outside of organizational channels; and, most importantly, work has shifted from manufacturing where value is added in the factory to services where value is added at the point of contact with the customer.[17]

The elemental conception of the firm has the advantage of simplifying the environment – the key decision criteria are what am I doing, what does it cost, who is the customer, and what is the customer willing to pay – even as the environment becomes more complicated. Whether or not firms can act on these criteria will depend on our capacity to deliver reliable cost and revenue information to our people. The contrast between the success many firms have had in cutting costs and their inability, so far, to understand the revenue consequences of the costs they incur suggests that the tools firms have used to manage costs, such as activity-based costing, could be transformed into performance measurement tools by applying them to both the revenue and the cost sides of the ledger. Just as activity-based costing reduces total costs to the costs of performing individual activities, can total revenues be reduced to revenues resulting from each of the activities performed by the firm?

Reductionism is an established principle in science. Modern science teaches us to reduce complex phenomena, whether physical systems or firms, to simpler elements in order to understand and control them. Often, of course, the simple questions raised by reductionist methods do not always admit of simple answers and sometimes they do not admit of any answers at all. This is especially true in the realm of management where we think of firms as more than the sum of their people and processes – firms have irreducible cultures, routines, reputations, and the like. But this does not mean that reductionist methods should not be tried, especially in performance measurement where the holistic approach may have created or compounded more problems than it has solved. This said, an important caution is in order: reducing firms to activities, costs, customers, and revenues may help us find better second-best measures, but it will not solve the underlying problem that all measures are second best. The gap between the performance we would like to measure and what we can measure can be narrowed, but it will not vanish.

A brief itinerary

This book addresses eight large questions: (1) What is meant by performance? (2) Is there an inherent gap between the prevailing conception of performance and our ability to measure performance? (3) Does this gap increase as firms grow larger and lags between actions and their economic results lengthen? (4) Do people exploit the gap between what we would like to measure and what we can measure, and how much does this affect the capacity of measures to discriminate good from bad performance? (5) Does the balanced scorecard correct the limitations and distortions inherent in almost all performance measures, does it compound these limitations and distortions, or does it create new ones? (6) Can we measure performance better by reducing the performance of the firm to the performance of its activities? (7) What are the strategic and managerial implications of reducing the performance of the firm to the performance of its activities? (8) Finally, and by implication, might the persistent gap between what we would like to measure and what we can measure ultimately prove advantageous even though it makes performance measurement difficult?

Chapter 1 raises some very basic issues about measurement and the performance of the firm. Modern performance measurement searches for what firms do that generates revenues in excess of costs. But, having set this agenda, performance measurement begins with the firm and its financial results, asks how the functioning of the parts of the firm shown on the organization chart contributes to these results, and then searches for measures of the functioning that predict financial results. This approach, I believe, goes awry due to a part-whole problem: it is difficult to connect measures of functioning that are dispersed throughout the organization with financial results accruing to the firm as a whole without losing a great deal of information.

Chapters 2 and 3 turn to the human element and why people's behavior renders performance measurement so challenging. One challenge lies in what people do when they are exposed to performance measures: they either improve actual performance or they improve measured but not actual performance, and it is all but impossible to tell the difference between the two unless you are measuring exactly what you want to accomplish (for firms, long-term economic results; for government and non-profit organizations what you want is less certain). The consequence is that measures are always in turmoil. Chapter 2 locates the source of this turmoil in the running down of performance measures, the tendency of almost all measures to lose variance and hence the capacity to discriminate between good and bad performance. Running down is attenuated in turbulent environments, but this creates a further complication for performance measurement: either you are in a placid environment where the variance of your measures collapses and leaves you unable to differentiate good from bad performance, or you are in a turbulent environment where your measures retain variance but the high level of uncertainty renders it difficult to predict the economic results you seek from the measures you have.

The human element also enters when we try to combine fundamentally different measures in order to appraise people's overall performance and compensate them. Many businesses have tried to appraise and pay their people using a combination of financial and non-financial measures suggested by the balanced scorecard. Chapter 3 reports on the efforts of a global financial services firm to compensate its people on both financial and non-financial measures in the 1990s. The company found that a formula-driven compensation system was susceptible to gaming, like any system where measures are fixed. Weighting measures subjectively, however, undermined people's motivation – they could not understand how they were paid. Since there is no middle ground between combining measures formulaically and combining them subjectively, the initial conclusion is that the balanced scorecard is not an effective performance measurement tool. This conclusion, however, does not mean that imbalance is a good thing. The same global financial services firm abandoned the balanced scorecard in 1999 and focused almost exclusively on sales performance. Compensating people on sales had the unintended consequence of accelerating customer attrition, most likely because customer service was ignored, even though revenues continued growing. Thus, while managers should understand the limits of the balanced scorecard and take care to distinguish the performance measurement from the strategic functions of the balanced scorecard, they should never forget that measuring performance in only one domain invites distortions in domains not measured.

Chapter 4 explores whether the main limitation of the balanced scorecard, the choice between subjective and formulaic weighting of dissimilar measures, can be overcome by developing comparable metrics for performance in different domains. Toward this end, the chapter shifts attention from the organization to the customer and ultimately the activity as the fulcrum of performance measurement. The chapter starts with a success story: when products or services are made to specifications known to add value for the customer, activities and the costs they incur can be removed and performance improved so long as specifications are not compromised. This observation is at the core of activity-based costing, and its application is responsible for many productivity improvements, especially in manufacturing. But can performance be similarly improved in settings where specifications adding value for the customer are not known? Or, more precisely, can performance be similarly improved where the activities incurring costs cannot be easily separated from the specifications adding value, which often occurs in services?

The chapter suggests that activity-based profitability analysis or ABPA, which is a revenue analog of activity-based costing, can help improve performance where specifications adding value for the customer are not known. ABPA uses the results of customer profitability analysis to estimate the profitability of different kinds of activities. What is important about ABPA is that it follows the performance chain, partitions the firm first by customers and revenues and then by activities and costs, and it then attaches costs to customers and revenues to activities. ABPA, in other words, is an alternative to following the organization chart, partitioning the firm into business units, functional units and work groups, and then trying to connect the firm's functioning, which occurs mainly in functional units and work groups, to the financial performance of business units and the firm as a whole.

Chapter 5 is about using ABPA, although it is hardly a "how to do it" guide. The chapter explores how firms using ABPA learn about the drivers of bottom-line performance and then compensate people's contribution to the bottom line. Learning takes place as experience accumulates and the drivers of customer profitability are revealed over time. People are then compensated on customer profitability, which can be driven deeper in the organization than conventional bottom-line measures.

Chapter 6 is about implementing ABPA. ABPA requires the firm to be designed around front-end customer units where activities, costs, customers, and revenues are joined. These customer units link back-end functional units, where many of the firm's activities and costs are incurred with customers who supply revenues to the firm. Customer units and their people are accountable for customer profitability. Functional units, in turn, support customer units by supplying products and services at costs and to specifications determined by customer units, but they are not directly responsible for customer profitability. This exercise in organizational design might not be important but for its consequences for forming and implementing strategy. Most of our thinking about strategizing assumes that strategy remains a senior management prerogative. The ABPA approach to performance measurement opens the possibility of decentralized strategizing, which nurtures strategizing capabilities at the local level where customers interface with firm. Decentralized strategizing capabilities, I argue, are especially important for global service firms offering huge arrays of products to multiple customer segments.

Some bedrock issues are beyond the purview of this book. Among them is whether we would be better off in a world where measurement is precise, that is, where measures correspond to the objectives we seek and people are compensated on these measures, or in a world where measurement is imprecise, where the correspondence between measures and objectives is imperfect and compensating people on these measures is problematic. There is no simple answer. There is a strong case for precision. A myriad of experimental studies demonstrate that motivation is strongest when people are given specific, challenging objectives. But the argument – I should say arguments – for imperfect measurement cannot be dismissed. The arguments for imperfection come from many sources, including Weber's *The Protestant Ethic and the Spirit of Capitalism*, where discipline and motivation come from *not* knowing what leads to salvation of the soul; from the notion of goal displacement, which suggests that the means organizations use to achieve their goals often become ends in themselves and hence deeply distorted; and from decades of research on command economies showing that quota systems lead to suboptimal performance because people anticipate that quotas once met will be raised; and from organizational theory and organizational economics, where it is taken for granted that firms pursue the dual objectives of efficiency, which can be measured, and adaptability, which cannot be.

The more immediate question addressed here is how firms will continue to improve performance as the business environment becomes more challenging. Most of the low-hanging fruit has been picked. Many of the performance gains of the 1990s were made by cutting costs and selling aggressively. Think, for example, of Jack Welch at General Electric or Sanford Weil at Citigroup. Whether the same strategy of treating costs and revenues as independent events – in the vernacular, cut costs on the one hand and drive revenues on the other – will work going forward is uncertain. The problem is not intent: when managers must cut costs, they seek to cut expenditures not contributing to revenues. The problem, rather, is that, absent analytic tools linking expenditures to revenues, the wrong costs are often cut. These analytic tools require a great deal of data, ideally data capturing all of the activities performed by the firm. Collecting these data and using these tools effectively, moreover, will require a rethinking of how the firm is organized and how it strategizes. This rethinking will allow firms simultaneously to pursue profit-maximizing strategies in front-end customer units and cost-minimizing strategies in back-end functional units.

The bottom line

For ease of review, each chapter will end with a condensation of its argument into a few bullet points.

- There is widespread dissatisfaction with existing performance measures.
- This dissatisfaction occurs because most performance measurement systems fail to meet some basic requirements, e.g. there should be relatively few measures, non-financial measures of functioning should predict financial performance, these measures should pervade the organization, they should be stable, and they should be used to appraise and compensate people's performance.
- While the balanced scorecard meets many of these requirements, it cannot be easily used to appraise and compensate people's performance. As a consequence, the scorecard has been recast as a framework for strategic management.
- Meeting the basic requirements of performance measurement is difficult because of the gap between how we would ideally measure a firm's performance, by connecting what a firm does with its future cash flows, or nearly equivalently its long-term viability and efficiency, and how we actually measure performance, by looking at measures of a firm's functioning and current financial results. This gap is exacerbated by a number of factors including large size, lengthy lags, and inertia in organizations, by the tendency of most measures to lose variance with use, and by the inherent difficulty of combining disparate functional and financial measures into an overall appraisal of performance. Much of this book concerns the fundamental properties of performance measures and factors exacerbating the problems of measuring performance.
- The performance chain and the elemental conception of the firm provide starting points for narrowing the gap between how we would ideally measure performance within the firm and how we currently measure performance: they locate performance in the activities

performed by the firm and measure performance by the cost and revenue consequences of these activities.

- A specific technique derived from activity-based costing, activity-based performance analysis or ABPA, is suggested as a means of implementing the performance chain and the elemental conception of the firm. ABPA measures costs and revenue consequences of activities and customer transactions performed throughout the firm.

- ABPA, though difficult to implement, combines fine-grained measurement of activities with measures of customer profitability. ABPA thus facilitates both learning about the drivers of financial performance and compensating people for bottom-line performance.

- ABPA changes how large service firms are managed. Under ABPA, the firm is organized around front-end customer units responsible for connecting the activities of back-end functional units and their costs with customers who supply revenues to the firm. Firms are thus able to pursue strategies of differentiation and customer profitability maximization in front-end customer units and cost minimization in back-end functional units simultaneously.

1 | Why are performance measures so bad?

A brief detour into abstraction may help illuminate why performance measures are often unsatisfactory and why performance measurement often proves frustrating, especially in large and complicated firms. Outside of the realm of business and economics, performance is what people and machines do: it is their functioning and accomplishments. This is codified in the dictionary. For example, The *Oxford English Dictionary* defines performance as:

> Performance. The action of performing, or something performed... The carrying out of a command, duty, purpose, promise, etc.; execution, discharge, fulfillment. *Often antithetical to promise* ... The accomplishment, execution, carrying out, working out of anything ordered or undertaken; the doing of any action or work; working, action (personal or mechanical); spec. the capabilities of a machine or device, now esp. those of a motor vehicle or aircraft measured under test and expressed in a specification... The observable or measurable behaviour of a person or animal in a particular, usu. experimental, situation... The action of performing a ceremony, play, part in a play, piece of music, etc....[1]

In other words, performance resides in the present (in the act of performing or functioning) or the past (in the form of accomplishments) and can therefore, at least in principle, be observed and measured. Performance is not in the future. To repeat the phrase I have italicized, performance is often "...antithetical to promise."[2]

Economic performance, by contrast, involves an element of anticipation if not promise. Following Franklin Fisher, the economic performance of the firm is "the magnitude of cash flow still to come,"[3] discounted to present value. This definition of economic performance can be easily generalized. Substitute efficiency for cash flow and allow discount rates to vary, even to fall below zero, and economic performance becomes the long-term efficiency and viability of a firm. What is important is that neither "cash flow still to come" nor long-term efficiency and viability are past actions or current accomplishments. Instead, they are outcomes of accomplishments and actions. As such, they will be revealed only as we move forward in time.

Note the tension between the dictionary definition and the economic definition of performance. The dictionary definition is current or backward looking, while the economic definition is forward looking. This tension plays out in different ways. In the day-to-day management of firms, we use the dictionary definition of performance by setting targets and comparing accomplishments to these targets, but we also use the economic definition of performance when driving measures of shareholder value into the firm. In academic research, we mix the dictionary and economic definitions of performance. The dictionary definition of performance is assumed where performance is measured by operational measures or current financial results, but the economic definition of performance is implicit in studies where performance is measured by share prices.

The dictionary and the economic definitions of performance – your past accomplishments and current functioning, and the future benefits resulting from accomplishments and functioning – are not tied to specific performance measures. But everyday definitions of performance tend to be more restrictive and closely tied to specific measures. For example, we can both define and measure the performance of the firm as profitability. Or we can both define and measure the performance of the firm as value delivered to shareholders. Alternatively, we can define performance as meeting requirements in the domains of financial results, operations, performance for the customer, and learning and innovation, in which case performance measures correspond to scorecard measures. Or we can define the performance of the firm as meeting the requirements of diverse stakeholder groups and gauge performance by stakeholders' appraisals of the firm's performance.

Note that we can array everyday notions of performance and performance measures along two dimensions, external versus internal and single versus multiple measures. The array looks something like table 1.1. Some common-sense propositions follow from this array. One proposition is that the more constituencies (both external and internal) and the greater their power, the more performance measures. It follows, for example, that organizations with more stakeholders will have more stakeholder measures. It also follows that the larger and more differentiated the organization, the more internal, that is

Table 1.1 *Everyday notions of performance and performance measures*

	External	*Internal*
Single measure	Example: shareholder value	Example: earnings, operating efficiency
Multiple measures	Example: stakeholder satisfaction	Example: balanced scorecard

scorecard-like, performance measures. Note that the balanced score-card (internal, multiple measures) turns out to be the internal counter-part of the multiple constituency model of the firm (external, multiple measures) where stakeholder satisfaction is paramount. Note also the meta-proposition: everyday performance measures reflect the diversity and power of actors in the organization and its environment. In other words, the organization and its environment are givens, and perfor-mance measures follow.

My perspective is different. I ask how we can improve performance measurement given the inherent limitations of performance measures rather than how we measure performance today given the constraints of the organization and its environment. Hence a central question con-cerns the deficiencies, the downsides, of everyday performance mea-sures. They are myriad. Consider the tradeoffs between single versus multiple measures. No single measure provides a complete picture of the performance of the organization. Moreover, things not measured will be sacrificed to yield better results on the things that are measured. It follows that the more things that are *not* measured, the more dis-tortion or gaming taking place in the organization. Multiple measures, by contrast, may yield a more complete picture of the performance of the organization than any single measure but are difficult to collect and combine into an appraisal of the overall performance of the orga-nization. Next, consider the choice tradeoffs external versus internal measures. External measures can be difficult to make operational and drive downward within the organization – how do you make the op-erative accountable for shareholder value? Correspondingly, internal measures can be difficult to roll up into an overall result that can be understood externally.

Given the endemic deficiencies of everyday performance measures – more on these deficiencies below – my concern is how they can be over-come, if only partially. Rethinking and simplifying the organization and its environment can remedy some of these deficiencies but not all of them. And no amount of rethinking and simplification will allow us to measure economic performance directly. This holds whether economic performance is construed narrowly as "cash flow still to come" or broadly as the long-term efficiency and viability of the organization.

Why all performance measures are second best

Performance as defined in the dictionary – accomplishments, functioning – can be observed directly and hence quantified, compared, and appraised. But economic performance, whether revenues not yet realized or the long-term efficiency and viability of the organization, cannot be observed and hence cannot be measured directly because it lies in the future. Economic performance must thus be inferred from measurable indicators of accomplishments or functioning. The indicators used to make inferences about economic performance may be financial (e.g. earnings or share prices) or non-financial (e.g. customer satisfaction). Though these indicators may predict (and if prediction is very good, appear to promise) economic performance, they remain indicators from which uncertain inferences about economic performance must be drawn rather than direct measures that gauge economic performance with certainty. *Absent first-best measures, all measures of economic performance are second best.* Some second-best measures, to be sure, will be better than others, but all performance measures are flawed so long as we are trying to measure economic performance or something akin to it.

The difference between the dictionary and economic definitions of performance brings us to performance measurement. Performance measurement bridges the dictionary and the economic definitions of performance by finding measures of accomplishments and functioning from which inferences about the future can be drawn. Measuring the accomplishments and functioning of a firm is not particularly difficult, but finding measures of accomplishments and functioning from which inferences about future cash flows or the long-term efficiency and viability of the organization can be drawn can be challenging. Moreover, such inferences are necessarily uncertain because they are always based on past economic performance. This is illustrated in figures 1.1 and 1.2. In figure 1.1, accomplishments, functioning, and economic performance are arrayed on a timeline. To understand figure 1.1, mentally

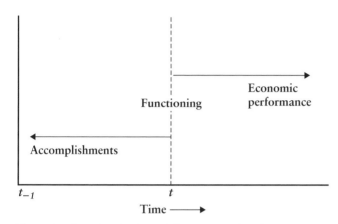

Figure 1.1 Location in time of three types of performance

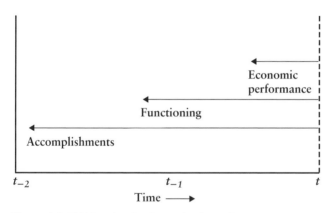

Figure 1.2 Shifting the timeframe backward

plant your feet at t, which represents today. Looking backward from t, you can observe recent accomplishments. Looking at the present, you can observe current functioning. Looking forward from t, however, you cannot observe economic performance because it has not yet been realized. Thus, without additional information, you are unable to draw inferences about economic performance from the functioning and accomplishments of a firm.

The additional information comes from past economic performance. Keep your feet planted at t, but shift the timeframe backward by focusing on economic performance up to t, which is measurable, functioning at t_{-1}, and accomplishments before that (figure 1.2). By shifting the timeframe backward in this way, you can observe and measure economic performance – that is, past economic performance. You can also measure past accomplishments and functioning. Performance measurement, then, connects the dictionary and the economic definitions of performance by shifting the timeframe backward and then asking how past accomplishments (including past financial performance) and functioning affected subsequent economic performance.

Defined in this way, performance measurement neither measures nor explains economic performance. Instead, it draws inferences about economic performance by looking forward to the present from the vantage of the past. Economic performance, however, lies ahead. Performance measurement is thus always surrounded by uncertainty because it depends on inference rather than direct measurement and observation. The amount of uncertainty varies with the lags between measures and their impact on economic performance, and the volatility of the business environment. This uncertainty notwithstanding, it is critical for firms to draw inferences about economic performance from the kinds of performance they can measure. Absent these inferences, firms would not know how well they are doing, and capital markets would not know how to value them. And absent these inferences, firms would be unable to improve their processes and, as a consequence, improve their economic performance.

It is also important to emphasize that not all measures of accomplishments and functioning are performance measures. The test of whether measures of accomplishments and functioning are also performance measures is this: did these measures predict economic performance in the past, and can they therefore reasonably be expected to predict future economic performance? Performance measurement, then, calls for more than quantifying the accomplishments, functioning, and economic performance of a firm. It also requires inferences to be drawn about economic performance from measured functioning and accomplishments. Whether valid inferences about economic performance can be drawn from the most widely used performance measures is a critical issue in performance measurement and a central issue of this book.

Some performance measures, though second best, are nonetheless quite good because reliable inferences about economic performance can be drawn from them. A measure from which reliable inferences are made routinely is the familiar fundraising thermometer, especially

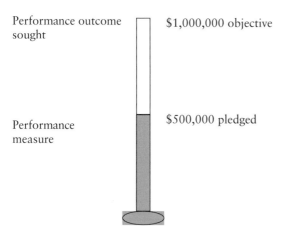

Performance outcome sought — $1,000,000 objective

Performance measure — $500,000 pledged

Figure 1.3 United Way thermometer

when used to chart the progress of an annual campaign such as United Way in the USA (see figure 1.3).[4] At the top of the thermometer is a goal, say $1 million (although some extra space may be left above the $1 million mark in case the goal is exceeded). At the beginning of the United Way drive, the thermometer reads zero. During the course of the campaign it rises. Should the thermometer reach the $500,000 mark toward the middle of the campaign and approach the $1 million toward the end, then the United Way campaign will be confidently said to be "on target." Should pledges fall significantly below these levels, then there will be calls for greater effort.

Note that the thermometer, while a second-best measure, is still a good performance measure. The thermometer is a second-best measure because it gauges progress toward the $1 million objective but does not predict with certainty whether this objective will be met (for example, all potential donors may be exhausted at the $500,000 mark due to changed economic conditions). On the other hand, the thermometer is a very good performance measure because it involves tacit comparisons with the past (progress to date in comparison with the goal this year versus progress to the same date in comparison with the goal last year) from which reliable inferences about the outcome of the campaign can be made. Note also that the United Way thermometer remains a very good measure only so long as the goals of the pledge drive change relatively little from year to year. Should a "stretch goal" be adopted at any point, that is, should the goal suddenly double or triple, then comparisons based on past experience might cease to yield reliable inferences about the current campaign.

By contrast with the United Way thermometer, promoters of mutual funds routinely make performance claims based on comparison of their past financial results with the financial results of competitors. Such comparisons are intended to suggest inferences about future financial results even though they are followed by the usual disclaimer that "past performance is not a guide to future returns." In this case, the disclaimer is more accurate than the inference drawn from past results – over the last two decades past results have been a very poor guide to future returns of mutual funds.[5] Indeed, the most parsimonious model of market behavior may be a random walk where successive price changes in a security are statistically independent.[6] The lesson here is that a measure, even a measure of past economic performance, does not contain information about current economic performance simply because differences exist on that measure. Rather, measures contain information about economic performance to the extent that inferences about economic performance can be drawn from them. The better these inferences, the better the measure, even though it is still a second-best measure.

How size and complexity complicate performance measurement

Performance measurement is complicated by large size and complexity in organizations. Imagine a firm so small that it cannot be reduced to still smaller units, a one-person, one-activity, one-product firm. Measures of the firm's functioning and its financial results describe the same unit, one person, making it easy for this person to plot financial results as a function of his or her functioning and hence to draw inferences about economic performance from measured functioning.

Performance measurement in an entrepreneurial firm

In small firms, it can be easy to draw inferences about economic performance from measures of functioning. Small firms, entrepreneurial firms especially, find it relatively easy to connect their functioning with financial results and hence to draw inferences about economic performance (provided, of course, they are not pioneering new technologies, in which case all bets are off).

Envirosystems Corporation leases sanitary waste treatment plants to mobile home parks, schools, shopping centers, military bases, golf courses, and large construction sites. The waste treatment business is a simple one despite the sizable dollars involved. There is no real competition. The technology is stable, modularized, and highly transportable, and Envirosystems' customers are extremely predictable. Finding customers is mainly a matter of scanning building permits for large projects not served by sewer mains, and then offering options to contractors bidding on the project. Retaining customers is even easier, since leases are non-cancelable. And the underlying economics of the business are extremely favorable: waste treatment plants have a service life of about twenty years, but can be depreciated in five to seven years and are often amortized over the initial one or two leases. Envirosystems, then, is a simple business even though its annual turnover is in the range of $100 million.

Envirosystems' owner, entrepreneur Ed Moldt operates more than 200 niche businesses whose total revenues exceed $1 billion annually. He manages these businesses by tracking three to five non-financial measures that are leading indicators of financial performance, setting targets on these measures, monitoring measures daily, rewarding people for performance so measured, and allowing the profits to take care of themselves. Moldt uses trial and error to find non-financial measures that are leading indicators of financial performance and usually hits on the right measures after two or three tries. Invariably, the right measures are unique to each business.[7]

The three performance measures Moldt uses to manage Envirosystems are the number of new leases, the number of terminating leases, and the number of postcards sent to consulting engineers newly listed in professional directories as specializing in sanitary waste. The number of leases in force (that is, existing leases plus new leases minus terminating leases) drives short-term revenues, and hence profitability because Envirosystems' operating costs are essentially fixed. The number of postcards sent to newly listed consulting engineers drives long-term revenues: the recipient typically files it and responds when a project requires temporary waste treatment facilities. Moldt also tracks Envirosystems' profitability – "I look at the bottom line all the time." But Moldt has found profitability to be redundant information because the number of new leases, terminating leases, and postcards predict revenues within 1–2 percent over the next five to eight years. Note that performance measures serve several purposes for Moldt. The number of new leases, terminating leases, and postcards look forward – they predict revenues. The bottom line looks backward – it captures past performance and allows Moldt to determine which non-financial measures predicted revenues. Moldt also uses measures to motivate his managers to perform and to compensate them for measured performance.

Performance measurement in a large firm

Drawing inferences about economic performance from measured accomplishments and functioning is relatively easy in small firms where measures are sparse to begin with, time lags are short, and organizational complexity does not impede intuitive mapping of measured accomplishments and functioning onto subsequent financial results. Large firms, however, have myriad measures, lengthy lags, and several layers of organization (from top to bottom, the firm, business units, functional units, and work groups) separating functioning from financial results. Publicly traded firms are understandably preoccupied with the valuation of their shares in capital markets. Firms more complicated than Envirosystems must also track myriad non-financial measures – it is not uncommon for large firms to have upward of 1000 operational measures. Inertia also increases with the size and complexity of the organization, extending the lags between a firm's functioning and its financial results.[8] Most importantly, non-financial and financial performance reside in different parts of the organization in large, complicated firms. Measures of functioning are scattered throughout the firm, while financial results accrue to the firm as a whole and its business units.

An internal study done by a global pharmaceutical firm illustrates how size (and, by inference, organizational complexity) affects the accuracy of revenue projections (and, by inference, performance measurement). The study plotted the accuracy of revenue forecasts for country businesses as a function of their size. The measure of size was prior year sales (in US dollars), while the measure of forecast accuracy was the absolute value of the percentage deviation of actual from projected sales in the current year. The data showed that forecast accuracy declined sharply with size – in other words, the deviation of actual from projected sales increased with the size of the business. This occurred even though the large country businesses used sophisticated modeling tools unavailable to the small businesses. There are many plausible explanations for this outcome, among them the possibility that revenue forecasts of the larger businesses were deliberately distorted by modeling tools. The simplest explanation, however, may be that trial-and-error methods like those used successfully by Ed Moldt worked well for the smaller country businesses but were never considered by the larger businesses due to their size and complexity.

Large, multi-level firms have tried to join measures of financial performance with measures of functioning in two ways. First, they have tried to cascade financial measures downward by breaking the organization into strategic business units and then by implementing metrics like EVA in each. Second, they have tried to roll up their measures of functioning from the bottom to the top of the organization by creating aggregate non-financial measures like overall customer satisfaction, average cycle time, and the like. These solutions, as will be shown, can be awkward, although they are less awkward when the firm can be partitioned into a large number of nearly identical business units – chain stores and franchises illustrate this kind of partitioning best. Firms that partition the organization into multiple and nearly identical business units requiring minimal coordination have had some success in cascading their financial measures downward and rolling up their non-financials from the bottom to the top of the organization. By contrast, firms whose units are specialized and highly interdependent have had the greatest difficulty cascading their financials downward and rolling up their non-financials from bottom to top.

Consider a stylized firm with four layers of organization: the *firm* as a whole; strategic *business units* that are essentially self-contained businesses; *functional units* (operations, marketing, sales, etc.) within business units; and *work groups* within functional units. The market valuation applies to the firm as a whole; financial performance is measured for the firm as a whole and for its business units. Revenues can be compared to expenses at these levels of the organization but cannot be compared at lower levels. By contrast, non-financial performance is measured in functional units and work groups because much of the functioning of the organization takes place at these lower levels.

Drawing inferences about economic performance from measured functioning, then, creates unique problems for large, multi-level firms because non-financial performance is measured in work groups and functional units while financial performance is measured in business units and the firm as a whole. Trial-and-error methods will not work in multi-level organizations, but analytic methods connecting non-financial measures with financial results require non-financial measures that roll up (that is, measures that can be summed or averaged) from work groups and functional units to business units and the firm as a whole, and financial measures that cascade down (that is, measures that can be disaggregated) from the firm and its business units to functional units and work groups.

It is true that analysts' earnings forecasts – as distinguished from internal revenue forecasts – are generally more accurate for large than small firms. This occurs for an interesting reason: analysts have access to more information about large firms than small ones due to superior collection and dissemination of data about large firms.[9] (By contrast, managers of small firms are likely to have better information about their businesses than their counterparts in large firms.) The proposition that the accuracy of earnings forecasts increases with the quantity and quality of data is nearly self-evident. But a corollary is not. Common sense suggests that CEO succession will degrade the accuracy of analysts' earnings forecasts because succession creates uncertainty. In fact, the opposite occurs: CEO turnover increases rather than degrades the accuracy of earnings forecasts because of the publicity accompanying the appointment of a new CEO.[10]

The seven purposes of performance measures

Large and complicated organizations, then, require more from their measures than smaller and simpler firms. In smaller and simpler firms, measures need only look ahead, look back, and motivate and compensate people. In larger and more complicated firms, measures are also expected to roll up from the bottom to the top of the organization, to cascade down from top to bottom, and to facilitate performance comparisons across business and functional units. These seven purposes of performance measures are illustrated in figure 1.4.

In figure 1.4, the look ahead, look back, motivate, and compensate purposes of performance measures are placed outside the organizational pyramid because they are common from the smallest and least formal to the largest and most organized firms. By contrast, the roll-up, cascade-down, and compare purposes, which become significant as firms grow in size and complexity, are placed within the pyramid because they are artifacts of organization. Second, look ahead and look

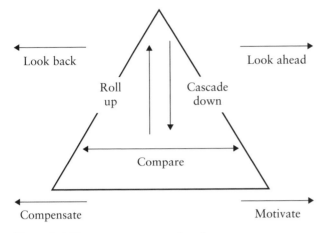

Figure 1.4 The seven purposes of performances measures

back are placed at the peak of the pyramid because measures having these purposes gauge the economic performance and past accomplishments of the firm as a whole, whereas motivate and compensate are at the bottom of the pyramid because measures having these purposes motivate and drive the compensation of individual people.

The four types of measures

Can any measures meet all of the requirements laid out in figure 1.4? To answer this question, think of the four types of measures: the valuation of the firm in capital markets (total shareholder returns, market value added), financial measures (accounting measures like profit margins, ROA, ROI, ROS, and cash flows), non-financial measures (for example, innovation, operating efficiency, conformance quality, customer satisfaction, customer loyalty), and cost measures. Then ask two questions: where in the organization is the performance gauged by measures of each type located, and which of the purposes shown in figure 1.4 do measures of each type fulfill?

Market valuation

Consider first measures of market valuation. The valuation of firms in capital markets gauges the performance of the entire firm but not business units, functional units or work groups, it looks ahead to the extent that financial markets are efficient and capture information pertinent to future cash flows, and it is widely used to motivate and compensate top executives. Since market valuation describes the performance of the firm but not its businesses, functions or work groups, it does not roll up from the bottom to the top of the organization nor can it be easily cascaded down from top to bottom, as illustrated by the response of the CFO of a global service when asked for his operating conception of shareholder value: "You probably know more about it, since you've thought about it more than I have."[11] Thus, even though market valuation greatly facilitates external performance comparisons, it does not facilitate internal comparisons because measures based on market valuation are difficult to drive down to the level of business or functional units.

Financial measures

Financial measures penetrate somewhat deeper into the organization and serve more purposes. Financial measures gauge the performance of the firm as a whole and its business units – units having income statements and balance sheets – but not functional units or work groups. In principle, financial measures look back rather than ahead because they capture the results of the past performance. In fact, current financial results also look ahead insofar as they affect the firm's cost of capital and its reputation – the better the results, the lower the cost of capital and the better the firm's reputation.[12] Financial measures, needless to say, are widely used to motivate people and drive their compensation. Financial measures roll up from individual business units (but not from functional units or work groups) to the top of the organization, cascade down from top to individual business units (but not to functional units or work groups), and facilitate performance comparisons across business units.

Non-financial measures

Non-financial measures are more complicated. On the one hand, non-financial performance is ubiquitous because it is the functioning of the firm, everything that the firm does, as distinguished from the financial results of what the firm does and the market valuation of these results. The consequence is a myriad of non-financial measures (for example, measures of new product development, operational performance, and marketing performance). On the other hand, since functional units within firms tend to be specialized, most non-financial measures of functioning will not apply across units having different functions (for example, measures gauging the speed of new product development will not apply to manufacturing and marketing units) and cannot easily be compared across functional units or combined into measures summarizing the performance of these units. The consequence is the following: first, non-financial measures gauge the performance of functional units but not the performance of its business units or of the firm as a whole. Second, non-financial measures capturing the functioning of the firm may or may not, depending on the measure, look ahead to future cash flows. In other words, some but not all non-financial measures look ahead, and there are no hard-and-fast rules for distinguishing non-financials that look ahead from those that do not. Third, non-financial measures believed to look ahead to future cash flows are used to motivate and compensate people – one would not motivate and compensate people on non-financial measures not believed to look ahead unless they were absolute "must-dos" such as safety. Fourth, most non-financial measures cannot easily be rolled up from the bottom to the top of the organization or cascaded down from top to bottom. Generally, the more specific the information about the firm's functioning contained in a non-financial measure, the more difficult it is to roll it up or cascade it down.[13] Fifth, non-financial measures can facilitate internal performance comparisons provided the same function is carried out at several points in the organization. Non-financial measures can also facilitate external comparisons where benchmark data are available.

Cost measures

Cost measures are limited in comparison with other types of measures because they measure performance incompletely – performance is more closely approximated by revenues in comparison with costs rather than by costs alone. Costs look back in the sense that costs tell you what you have spent. The trajectory of costs, of course, looks ahead. Failure to control costs will have adverse consequences for the organization. Cutting costs can have either favorable or unfavorable consequences depending on which costs are cut – chapter 4 begins with a case where cutting costs by eliminating the quality function would have had disastrous consequences for the organization. And costs are not normally used to motivate or to compensate people, although they can be so used when cost control is critical. Cost measures do have two interesting properties, however. First, costs penetrate the organization more deeply than other types of measures. Costs can be readily rolled up from the working level of the organization to the top and cascaded down from top to the working level, even though hard and fast rules for allocating costs do not always exist. Indeed, activity-based costing allows costs to be disaggregated to the level of individual activities performed by the firm. And costs can be compared laterally across any level of the organization regardless of the functions performed at that level.

Comparing the four types of measures

Table 1.2 compares the four types of performance measures with respect to where performance they measure is located in the organization and the purposes served by measures of each type. The table shows that measures that actually or potentially look ahead – measures from which inferences about economic performance can be drawn – usually do not roll up or cascade down the organization. Specifically, the market valuation of the firm does not cascade down the organization easily, and measures of the firm's functioning do not roll up easily. As a result, it is difficult to find measures applying across different levels of the organization from which inferences about economic performance can be made. Financial measures look ahead only in the short term, roll up from business units to the firm as a whole and cascade down from the firm to business units, but do not penetrate to functional units and work groups. Some non-financial measures look ahead, although many do not, and most have neither roll-up nor cascade-down capability. Finally, cost measures do not look ahead, although the trajectory of costs does, and can be easily rolled up from work groups to functional units, business units, and the firm as a whole and cascaded down from the firm to work groups.

Given that all measures have strengths and limitations, managers would like guidance as to what kinds of measures are best. What evidence there is does not provide a great deal of guidance. On the one hand, analysts' earnings forecasts often ignore basic information contained in financial statements[14] as well as more sophisticated measures like EVA,[15] current dividends,[16] competitors' earnings,[17] and the like. On the other hand, according to research done by Ernst & Young's Center for Business Innovation, analysts tend to weight non-financial measures more heavily than is generally supposed, but the weights

Table 1.2 *Types of measures by locus and purposes served*

	Market valuation	Financial measures	Non-financial measures	Cost measures
Levels where measures apply	Firm	Firm business units	Functional units	Firm business units; functional units; work units
Purposes served by measures				
Look ahead	+	? (short-term)	+(long-term, but which?)	? (trajectory of costs may look ahead)
Look back		+		+
Motivate	+ (mainly TMT)	+(mainly TMT and business managers)	+	
Compensate	+ (mainly TMT)	+(mainly TMT and business managers)	+	
Roll up		+(from business units to firm)	?	+
Cascade down		+(from firm to business units)	?	+
Compare		+(across business units)	?	+

Note: TMT = top management team.

attached to different non-financial measures vary dramatically from industry to industry. For example, strength in new product development is weighted more heavily in pharmaceuticals than in other industries. Moreover, the greater the importance of intangible assets, as in technology and internet-related industries, the more weight is attached to non-financial measures.[18]

The paradox of large organizations

All of this translates readily into managerial language. Managers expect measures to look ahead so that inferences about economic performance can be drawn from them. Managers also expect measures to roll up and cascade down the organization so that people at different levels will act in concert. (This is called *alignment* or "line of sight.") This analysis suggests that the types of measures that look ahead – mainly market valuation and non-financial measures – tend not to have roll-up and cascade-down capability, whereas measures having roll-up and cascade-down capability – mainly financial and cost measures – tend not to look ahead. This then is the paradox of large organizations. Firms grow because they are successful, but as they grow they specialize internally. The result of specialization is that many kinds of functioning and many measures of functioning are dispersed throughout the organization. In order to make inferences about economic performance, these dispersed measures of functioning must somehow be connected with financial results accruing at the level of the firm or its business units. While it is possible to draw inferences about economic performance from the measured functioning of small firms, as the case of Envirosystems shows, this becomes much more difficult as firms grow in size and complexity and their functioning no longer takes place in the units where financial results accrue.

At this point, it may be useful to go back to the United Way thermometer in figure 1.3 and ask why large firms cannot operate like a United Way drive by setting a specific goal, measuring progress toward this goal at all levels of the organization, and holding individual people accountable for progress toward this goal; in other words, why do large firms have difficulty following the precepts of textbook motivation theory when deciding performance measures? There are two reasons. First, like the United Way drive, firms can set only short-term, measurable objectives to motivate people, whereas unlike the $1m objective of the United Way campaign, the economic performance firms seek extends into the future and is beyond measurement. Second, like the United Way drive, firms would like to cascade measures from the top to the bottom of the organization, but unlike the United Way drive firms find this very difficult to do because of the complexity of the organization itself – it is difficult, for example, to find measures connecting what front-line workers do with shareholder value.

We yearn for simplicity in performance measurement. But we also seek the benefits of specialization and construct complex organizations to reap these benefits. Thus, while finding performance measures that look ahead, look back, motivate, compensate, roll up, cascade down, and facilitate performance comparisons is relatively easy in settings like the United Way where objectives are short-term and specific, it is a much more daunting task in organizations seeking long-term economic performance that are of substantially greater size and complexity.

How firms have sought to improve measurement

The paradox of large organizations – firms succeed, grow, specialize internally, disperse their functioning, and then find it difficult to connect measures of functioning with financial results and long-term economic performance – is at the core of the performance measurement problems many firms experience. Few firms, however, recognize the extent to which the requirements of organization have contributed to the performance measurement problem. They view the problem as measurement, and the solution as finding better measures. Specifically, they look for measures of market valuation and financial measures that can be readily cascaded down from the top of the organization, and non-financial measures that can be rolled up from bottom to top just as readily to link non-financial measures with bottom-line financial results.

Driving financial measures downward

Firms have persistently tried to drive financial measures to the lowest possible level of the organization. This effort began in the 1920s when large firms such as General Motors and DuPont replaced their unitary organizations with multiunit organizations that divided the larger firm into business units responsible for bottom-line performance. By the

1960s, reorganization of the firm along the lines of the multiunit was widely accepted as the solution to the problems of measuring operational efficiency and promoting efficiency in the allocation of capital, and few unitary organizations remained.

The multiunit firm as a tracking mechanism

In unitary firms, the central office coordinated the activities of functional subunits such as manufacturing and sales, tracked costs and operational performance in detail, but had no common measures with which to compare the performance of subunits. In multiunit firms, by contrast, the central office coordinated strategic planning, monitored the performance of subunits engaged in different lines of business using common financial measures, and allocated capital to business units based on financial performance. In effect, the central office managed the firm as an internal capital market, one potentially more efficient than external capital markets because of its power to inspect and, if necessary, intervene in individual business units. Figure 1.5 compares the organization and performance measures of primitive unitary and multiunit firms. The unitary firm shown in figure 1.5 has three functions, purchasing, production, and sales, while the multiunit firm has three business units (whether units differ by product, geography, or customers is immaterial), each having the same functions as the unitary organization. (Staff functions such as accounting are omitted for the sake of simplicity.) The performance measures available to these primitive firms differ dramatically. In the unitary firm, there are several measures, none common to all three units. The performance of the purchasing function is gauged by costs and availability of raw materials; the performance of manufacturing is gauged by capacity utilization, down time, and defects; and sales performance is gauged by gross sales less returns. Absent common measures, there is no way to compare the performance of the purchasing, manufacturing, and sales units, there is no rational way to allocate resources among these units, and the firm's performance suffers as a consequence.

Consider now the multiunit firm. Because multiunits have common performance measures, revenues and earnings in figure 1.5, performance can be compared across business units, resources can be allocated rationally among units, and the performance of the firm is enhanced as a consequence. As Oliver Williamson has observed: "*The organization and operation of the large enterprise along the lines of*

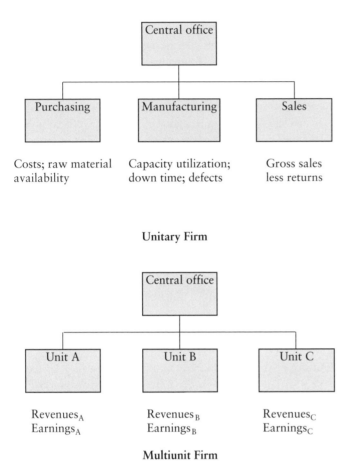

Figure 1.5 Organizational design and performance measures of unitary and multiunit firms

the M-form [multiunit form] *favors goal pursuit and least-cost behavior more nearly associated with the neoclassical profit maximization hypothesis than does the U-form* [unitary form] *organizational alternative.*"[19]

The advantages of multiunit firms, however, have proved temporary. Firms have grown, and the problems experienced by unitary firms have reappeared within business units of multiunit firms. Indeed, from the mid-1970s on, there have been indications that driving financial measures downward from the firm as a whole to its business units postpones but does not solve performance measurement problems caused by large size and complexity. In 1976, Louis Gerstner (former chairman of IBM) and A. Helen Anderson argued that the financial measures used to gauge the performance of business units were artificially constructed and possibly worthless:

> In many corporations during the 1960s . . . earnings per share – on a yearly, quarterly, or even monthly basis – was the name of the game . . . Today, many of these same companies recognize that short-term EPS data can be misleading as an index of a company's true strength and, by the same token, that a somewhat arbitrarily constructed profit figure may be worthless as a performance measure for a department or division of a decentralized organization. In short, measuring current profit performance, though obviously still important, is no longer sufficient. This is why a growing number of companies have begun to monitor a broader set of variables: in particular, asset intensity, return on investment, and non-accounting data.[20]

Today, of course, dissatisfaction with performance measures is endemic – most measures are believed deficient, not just business-unit level financial measures.

Economic value added

From the beginning of the stock market boom in the early 1980s onward there have also been efforts to drive market valuation from the level of the firm to business units and below. Few firms attempt to disaggregate the market valuation of their shares into market valuations for their business units. Many firms do, however, attempt to compare the rates of return generated by their business units with market rates of return. The measure that has gained the widest acceptance in the business community because it appears to come closest to measuring whether returns are above, at, or below market is economic value added or EVA, which has been trademarked by Stern, Stewart & Co. Joel Stern, a principal of Stern, Stewart, argues that EVA offers a better measure of returns relative to the market or residual income than conventional accounting measures:

> Incentivizing management to increase shareholder value means nothing to management unless the executives understand how value is created. Shareholder value depends largely on two basic factors: (1) the rate of return earned on total investor capital relative to the required rate of return, known as the "cost of capital," and (2) the amount of investor capital tied up in the business.

Shareholder value is created only when the rate of return on capital (r) exceeds the cost of that capital (c). The precise amount of value added is equal to the amount of total capital invested (TC) multiplied by the difference between r and c. In essence, this is best described as "residual income" – the only internal measure of corporate performance to tie directly to value. We like to refer to it as economic value added (EVA).[21]

The two key components of EVA, earnings and capital costs, are publicly available. What renders EVA unique is an adjustment of earnings that involves up to 160 factors, the comparison of adjusted earnings with capital costs, and the ranking of firms by EVA in Stern, Stewart's "Performance 1000." EVA has drawn many encomiums from the business press. In 1993, for example, *Fortune* proclaimed EVA "the real key to creating wealth."[22] More recently, *Fortune* announced that EVA has displaced EPS as the critical performance metric for many firms:

> For years, earnings per share has been the most popular girl at the party . . . Hundreds of companies, from AT&T to Brahma Beer, have renounced EPS and her whole GAAP family as a means of measuring performance . . . Wall Street, no slouch, is also jumping on the bandwagon: CS First Boston has trained its research staff in EVA analysis, and Goldman Sachs is about to introduce EVA . . .[23]

While EVA measures residual income rather than earnings, it is not clear that EVA contains information about economic performance not contained in earnings or standard financial ratios like return on assets (ROA). The small number of academic studies now available suggest that EVA contains little unique information. Using Stern, Stewart's "Performance 1000" data, Gary Biddle, Robert Bowen and James Wallace find, for example, that earnings are better predictors of share values than EVA: "all of the evidence points to earnings having at least equal (and often higher) relative information content [than EVA]."[24] James L. Dodd and Shimin Chen, also using the Stern, Stewart database, report that while EVA is somewhat predictive of share prices, ROA is a much better predictor.[25] The problem with EVA appears not to be susceptibility to short-run manipulation of its earnings component since, according to Dodd and Chen, earnings and ROA are subject to the same manipulations. It remains possible, of course, that EVA looks forward to future cash flows better than current earnings or ROA, but its failure to predict share prices as well as accounting ratios like ROA suggests that it may not.

*Placing non-financial measures on an equal footing with
financial measures*

Paralleling efforts to drive financial measures downward, firms have
tried to place non-financial measures – measures gauging a firm's
functioning, including operational measures, marketing measures, and
customer measures – on an equal footing with financial measures.
Increased top-level attention to non-financial measures has been motivated by the belief that both financial and non-financial measurement
are needed to convey the full picture of the firm's performance.

The balanced scorecard approach

The initial impetus for non-financial measurement came from the quality movement and, in particular, the Malcolm Baldrige award competition, which encouraged firms to measure and report employee morale,
product quality, and customer satisfaction. More recently, the impetus
for non-financial measurement has come from Kaplan and Norton's
notion of the balanced scorecard, where balance is defined as measurement in the domains of innovation, internal process, customer satisfaction, and financial performance. The balanced scorecard is particularly
significant because it has diffused rapidly and is now used for purposes
other than those originally intended. Although the scorecard was con-
ceived as a means of communicating the firm's strategy rather than as
a template for performance measurement, today the scorecard domi-
nates discussions of performance measurement, and compensation is
routinely based on scorecard measures. Chapter 3 will look at the use
of the balanced scorecard in compensation.[26]

Business models of performance

In order to place non-financial measures on an equal footing with financial measures, firms have had to construct business models sketching
plausible linkages between financial and non-financial performance.
To illustrate a fairly complicated business model: product quality increases customer satisfaction, which contributes to market share; market share, in turn, promotes profitability through increased revenues
and decreased unit costs; and profitability improves share prices, yielding gains in employee commitment and investment and hence gains in
product quality.[27] Business models of performance need not be circular

as in this instance but may, instead, may be sequential and terminate with an outcome state such as shareholder value. Whether circular or sequential, business models usually specify relationships among constructs such as product quality and customer satisfaction. These constructs assume that the non-financial performance of a firm can be reduced to a relatively small number of constructs and summary measures of these constructs.

It turns out that the constructs used in even the simplest business models raise some subtle but very important performance measurement issues. A business model used by Sears, Roebuck and Company called the employee-customer profit chain illustrates these issues.[28] The idea motivating the employee-customer profit chain was that Sears' profitability depended on its being a compelling place to work and a compelling place to shop. The model reduced to a formula: *work* × *shop = invest*. Measures of employee satisfaction and customer satisfaction were used to gauge whether Sears was a compelling place to work and shop. An initial set of seventy employee measures was reduced to ten measures and two constructs – six measures of attitude about the job (e.g. "I like the kind of work I do"), and four measures of attitude about the company (e.g. "I feel good about the future of the company") – assumed to reflect the quality of management because they predicted employee behaviors associated with customer satisfaction. The model was predictive of financial outcomes for 800 Sears stores over two quarters. An increase in employee attitudes of 5 units led to a 1.3 unit increase in customer satisfaction which, in turn, produced a 0.5 percent increase in revenue growth.[29] The model was also folded into Sears' compensation plan. Beginning in 1996, long-term incentives were based one-third on employee satisfaction, one-third on customer satisfaction, and one-third on traditional investor measures.

The performance measurement issue raised by Sears' employee-customer profit chain is this: employee satisfaction and customer satisfaction are performance measures in that they carry implications for Sears' economic performance. Sears' business results leave no doubt about that, at least for the stores and the time period covered by the research. But the performance – performance as defined in the dictionary – that adds value for customer, and hence profits Sears, is not employee and customer satisfaction. This performance, instead, lies in

managerial and employee actions captured only indirectly in employee
satisfaction and customer satisfaction. Thus, while Sears understands
that employee and customer satisfaction are drivers of profitability, it
cannot attach costs to employee and customer satisfaction because it
does not know what actions produce them and the cost of these actions.
Sears thus runs the risk that by continuing to measure and reward employee and customer satisfaction, the company will over-invest in employee and customer satisfaction, which will at some point be improved
at a cost exceeding its economic benefit. Put plainly, there are behaviors
that will satisfy employees and customers while sacrificing profits, and
focusing attention on employee and customer satisfaction runs the risk
of eliciting these behaviors. More generally, all non-financial measures
removed from actions taken by people run similar risks – again, people
can meet targets on these measures by taking actions that manifestly
do not add value in excess of the costs they incur.

The proliferation of measures

A consequence of driving financial measures downward in the firm and
placing non-financial measures on an equal footing with financial measures has been a glut of performance measures. The glut of measures
is best illustrated by comparing measures of the 1960s with measures
typical of the 1990s. Figures 1.6 and 1.7 array measures of the 1960s
and 1990s in two dimensions. The horizontal dimension represents
the most commonly used categories of measurement – innovation and
new product development (development), human resources (people),

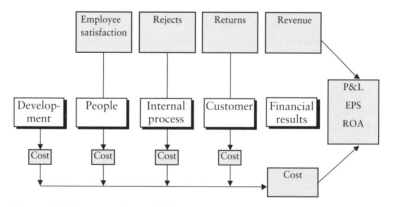

Figure 1.6 Measures circa 1960

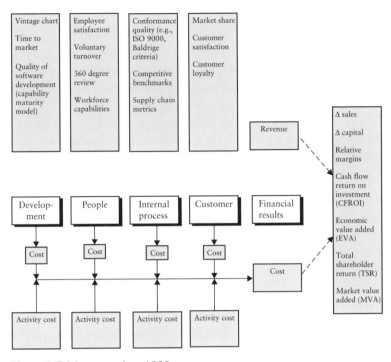

Figure 1.7 Measures circa 1990

process, customer, and financial results. The vertical dimension separates measures of functioning from cost measures in four of the five categories, product development, people, internal process, and customer. At the far right are financial and market measures, which arise from comparisons of revenues with costs.[30]

The explosion of non-financial measures

There are many differences between measures of the 1960s and the 1990s, but some of the most significant are as follows. To begin, while there were many more measures in the 1990s than the 1960s, the burgeoning of non-financial measures from the 1960s to the 1990s is especially noticeable. Measures of functioning were very sparse in the 1960s and were understood as principally cost drivers rather than revenue drivers. Low morale, for example, caused costly employee turnover, rejects contributed to manufacturing costs, and returned goods incurred costs that had to be written off. By contrast, not only were there many more measures of functioning in the 1990s compared to the 1960s, but measures of functioning were also understood differently, as leading indicators of revenues rather than as drivers of costs. To illustrate: time to market was believed to predict profit margins (the less time to market, the higher the margins), the ratio of new products to all products shown on vintage charts was believed to predict the sustainability of profits, and employee satisfaction was believed to contribute to customer satisfaction, the latter understood as an indicator of the firm's reputation and hence a predictor of the volume of both new and repeat business.

The preoccupation with market valuation

A comparison of figures 1.6 and 1.7 reveals another significant change in measures from the 1960s to the 1990s: the shift toward measures capturing the market valuation of the firm and financial measures believed to influence market valuation. Two key market valuation measures used in the 1990s were total shareholder return (TSR), dividends plus appreciation as a percentage of market valuation at the beginning of the period, and market value added (MVA), the difference between the market's current valuation of the firm and the firm's historical capital investment.[31] EVA, already discussed, and cash flow return on investment (CFROI), cash flows relative to the inflation-adjusted cost of capital, are residual income measures that in theory if not in practice gauge performance relative to capital costs and should be reflected in market valuations. Relative margins reflect a firm's advantage or disadvantage vis-à-vis competitors, growth of capital indicates the trajectory of capital costs that will impair or improve performance depending on the rate of return on capital, and sales growth reflects the trajectory of the business.

The emphasis on costs

Another change from the 1960s to the 1990s was the introduction of activity-based costing (ABC), especially in manufacturing. ABC drove costing very deeply into the organization by identifying the actual costs of labor, equipment, and premises associated with each activity performed by the firm rather than relying on arbitrary formulas to allocate overhead. We will look closely at ABC and its implications for performance measurement in chapter 4.

The compression principle in measurement

Taken singly, most of the measures of the 1990s make sense. Together, however, they may not. Measurement is not measuring more. Measurement, rather, compresses or condenses information by ordering what would otherwise be unordered bits of data so as to focus on critical properties of the object at hand. This principle can be demonstrated by considering the infinite number of points on a line. When we measure the length of the line, we are concerned only with the distance between the two end points. Nothing else is relevant – neither the distance between the other points nor the location of the line – that is, the location of its infinite points in space – is relevant to its length. *New York Times* science writer George Johnson explains the compression principle as follows: "We partition the universe into an area of interest and an environment to which we can banish excess information. And so we can make rough predictions. Iguses [information-gathering-and-utilizing systems] exist by virtue of this myopia, this inherent inability to keep track of every detail...If you know everything, you know nothing."[32] The compression principle is also understood by consultants who view the proliferation of measures shown in figures 1.6 and 1.7 as evidence of "measurement disintegration," that is, our capacity to produce performance measures faster than we can distinguish those measures containing information about economic performance from those that do not.[33]

The challenge of simplifying measurement

Performance measurement, as we have seen, involves making inferences about economic performance, which cannot be observed and measured because it lies ahead, from what can be observed and measured. Such inferences are needed for firms to appraise how well they are doing and to improve what they are doing, and for capital markets to value firms. In order to make such inferences we are compelled to rely on past experience, which means that our inferences about economic performance going forward will always be uncertain. This uncertainty means that we can never be confident that we have the right measures. Uncertainty is endemic in performance measurement, and there is very little we can do about it.

Our ability to make inferences about economic performance is limited by two further factors: the vast array of performance measures that now exist and the difficulty of cascading standard financial measures from the top to the bottom of the organization while rolling up a large number of non-financial measures from the bottom to the top. These problems are minimal in firms that have few layers and the ability to use trial-and-error methodology to converge on a few non-financial predictors of financial results quickly. Envirosystems, which is small and highly focused, illustrates this type of firm. These problems can also be minimized in large, multi-layered firms provided they can be partitioned into large numbers of similar business units with common performance measures. Sears, whose 800 retail outlets use standard measures of employee and customer satisfaction, is an example of this type of firm.

Firms that are larger and less focused than Envirosystems and cannot be partitioned into hundreds of similar business units like Sears face the challenge of simplifying their measures – of compressing many measures into few – before they can begin to make reasonable inferences about their economic performance from what they can measure. This simplification will occur in one of two ways. Some large firms will devolve into smaller, nimbler firms like Envirosystems or will be replaced by smaller, nimbler firms. Firms that remain large in order to realize scale or scope economies, for example, consumer product and financial service firms, may take a very different path by partitioning themselves into units that are minuscule in comparison with the units now shown on organization charts and then applying common measures to these units. As suggested in the introduction, this partitioning might take place activity by activity and customer by customer provided that revenues and costs can be linked at the level of activities and customers. In chapters 4 and 5 we will examine whether these linkages can be established, specifically whether revenues can be assigned to activities and costs assigned to customers once activity costs and customer revenues are known.

Before addressing this issue, chapters 2 and 3 will explore other vulnerabilities of performance measures that compound the problem of making inferences about economic performance from what we can measure. One vulnerability lies in what people do to measures. Almost all conventional performance measures are susceptible to running down, that is, loss of variance, which ultimately makes it difficult to discriminate good from bad performance. Another vulnerability surfaces when we try to use several performance measures to appraise people's performance and compensate them based on this appraisal. Combining disparate non-financial and financial measures into an overall performance appraisal turns out to be unexpectedly difficult because there are no good choices – measures are either combined by formula, in which case people will game the formula, or they are combined subjectively, in which case people are demotivated because they do not know how they are compensated.

The bottom line

Although this chapter was mainly conceptual, four key points should be taken away:

- Performance measures are intended, among other things, to give us insight into the future, the long-term economic performance of the firm, which is beyond the reach of measurement. All performance measures, as a consequence, are imperfect indicators of an uncertain future. Still, some measures are better than others.
- The larger and more complicated the firm, the greater the imperfection of performance measures. This occurs for several reasons: there is a more intensive division of labor and hence more measures of functioning in large firms than in small firms; the time lags between the actions taken by a firm and their economic consequences tend to be longer in large than in small firms (although lags can be very long in small firms with unproven technologies); and, most importantly, the functioning of large firms is dispersed across specialized units whereas financial results accrue to its businesses and the firm as a whole, making it difficult to connect the two.
- Firms have sought to improve performance measurement by cascading financial measures from the top to the bottom of the organization, rolling up non-financial measures from the bottom to the top, and seeking new measures thought to contain information not in existing measures. The strategy of cascading financials downward while rolling up non-financial measures has been successful mainly in firms partitioned into large numbers of homogeneous business units. For other firms, this strategy has resulted in a glut of measures.

- To reduce this glut of measures, large firms may have to partition themselves into units much smaller than those now shown on organization charts, specifically activities (which incur costs) and customers (who supply revenues). By partitioning the firm activity by activity and customer by customer and then assigning costs to customers and revenues to activities, it may be possible to construct a performance chain connecting what a firm does with its costs and revenues, and hence with its financial performance.

2 | *The running down of performance measures*

T HIS chapter introduces the role of people in performance measurement. It explores how performance measures change as people use them. The focus, in other words, is more on what people do to measures than what measures do to people. The underlying argument is that what measures do to people causes people to behave in ways that erode the capacity of measures to discriminate good from bad performance. This phenomenon compounds the problems of measuring performance laid out in chapter 1. Managers thus face two challenges when considering performance measures. The first is finding performance measures that contain information about cash flows still to come. The second challenge is examining their measures continuously and replenishing them as existing measures deteriorate.

This chapter is grounded in several premises. The first we have already encountered: all performance measures are second-best indicators of an uncertain future, although some second-best measures are better than others. The second premise is common sense, but with a twist: people will generally improve what is measured, and sometimes, people will improve what is measured without improving the underlying performance that is sought. It can be difficult to distinguish improvement in the measure from improvement in performance because the performance that is sought lies in the future and cannot be measured directly. The third premise will be demonstrated presently: improvement in what is measured, with or without accompanying improvement in performance, usually shrinks differences in measured performance and hence in the capacity of measures to discriminate good from bad performance as well. I call this diminution of differences the *running down* of performance measures. It is the use-it-and-lose-it principle in performance measurement. A fourth premise follows from the third: as existing measures run down, new measures capable of discriminating good from bad performance are sought. The result is that performance measures never stand still. Instead, firms change their performance measures continuously and sometimes abruptly.

My approach in this chapter is eclectic. I take measures from wherever I can get them, sometimes from business but often not, to illustrate running down. Since there are more baseball statistics in the USA than statistics of any other kind, one of the key examples is from that sport. But there are also examples from hospitals, the nuclear power industry, public bureaucracies, education, money market mutual funds, commercial banks, quality ratings in the automotive industry, and the market for initial public offerings. I use the example of one company, General Electric, to demonstrate that stellar firms can and do shift their measures dramatically, but I also draw a large database describing many companies to illustrate that performance measures are more often disparate than consistent.

Why performance measures run down

The running down of performance measures is nearly ubiquitous. Running down occurs when differences in measured performance diminish to such a degree that it is no longer possible to discriminate good from bad performance. Running down, as will be shown, has several causes, and it can be difficult to distinguish among them. These causes include positive learning, perverse learning, selection, suppression, and social consensus.

Positive learning

Batting averages in major league baseball

Many performance measures lose their ability to convey information about performance because their variability declines as performance improves. Perhaps the most vivid illustration of running down due to positive learning comes from the history of batting averages in major league baseball, which has been documented by paleontologist Stephen Jay Gould.[1] The facts are straightforward: from 1876 through 1980, there was virtually no change in the mean batting average, which hovered consistently around .260, plus or minus ten points. Over the same time period, however, *variance* in batting averages eroded substantially. This is illustrated in figures 2.1–2.2. Figure 2.1 displays differences between the five highest individual batting averages and the mean batting

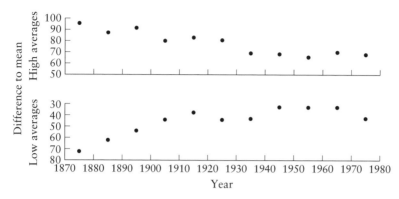

Figure 2.1 Differences between mean batting averages and batting averages for highest and lowest 10 percent of major league players

average by decade; the lower half of the figure shows differences between the five lowest averages and the overall mean. The two trends are symmetrical: both differences diminish over time, yielding sharply decreasing spreads between high and low averages. Figure 2.2 displays standard deviations of major league regular players' batting averages for the 105-year interval. The pattern is consistent with figure 2.1, as standard deviations decrease regularly over time. Gould asserts that the trend toward decreased variance reflects "an excellence of play"[2] as both batters and pitchers approach the "right wall" of human limits.[3] Clearly, improvement has taken place on both sides of the plate, causing variation in batting averages to shrink. This has rendered batting averages progressively less useful as a measure of performance so that, today, slugging averages and indexes of run production have largely displaced simpler batting averages in contract negotiations,[4] and ballplayers' salaries no longer correspond even remotely to their batting averages.[5]

Hospitals

The case of batting averages appears to be one where diminished variances surrounding a constant mean are caused by improved proficiency. The experience of hospitals is more complicated than batting averages in that diminished variance is attributable to multiple causes: improvement in some performance measures, stability in others, and deterioration in still other measures. Three widely used measures of hospital performance illustrate three patterns. Of the three measures considered

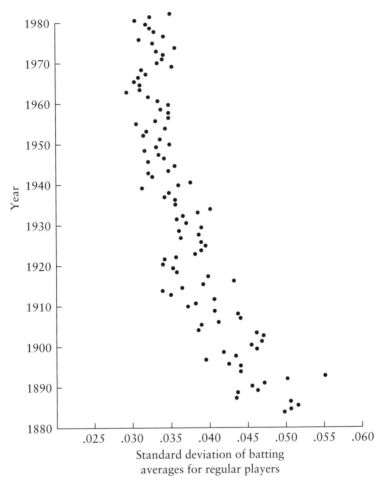

Figure 2.2 Standard deviation of batting averages by year

here, one, average length of stay (figure 2.3), exhibits a strong downward trend (which today is understood as improvement but was not
always). A second measure, cost per in-patient day (figure 2.4), exhibits
a strong upward trend (which today is understood as deterioration but
was not always). A third measure, occupancy rate (figure 2.5), remains
essentially flat over time (neither improving nor deteriorating by any
standard). The data are displayed in two ways in each of these figures,
as raw numbers in the upper panels (save that the cube root of cost

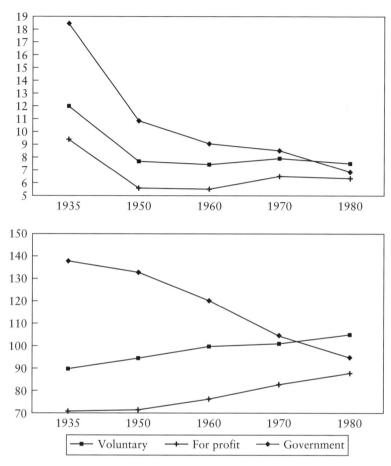

Figure 2.3 Average length of patient stay for voluntary, for-profit, and government hospitals by year (actual/normalized)

per in-patient day has been taken in the upper panel of figure 2.4), and in normalized form so that the means of the three measures remain at 100 throughout the series in the lower panels. The plots show persistent diminution in variance or convergence in performance measures across the three principal types of hospitals in the USA. The tendency is especially strong when the data are displayed in normalized form. Convergence is strongest for length of stay and cost per in-patient day and somewhat weaker for occupancy rate (where some divergence occurred between 1970 and 1980), but these results are

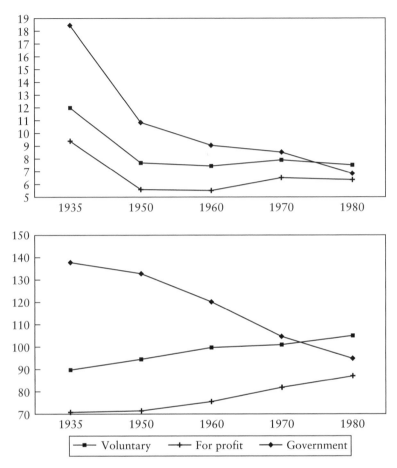

Figure 2.4 Average cost per in-patient day for voluntary, for-profit, and government hospitals by year (actual/normalized)

especially remarkable given that overall trends are in the direction of improvement for length of stay but deterioration in cost per in-patient day.

Nuclear power plants
Safety statistics of US nuclear power plants from 1985 through 1989 also exhibit diminished variance over time, which, like batting averages in major league baseball, is due almost entirely to improvement.[6] A consistent pattern occurs across five safety-related measures – scrams (automatic reactor shutdowns), safety system actuations, occurrences

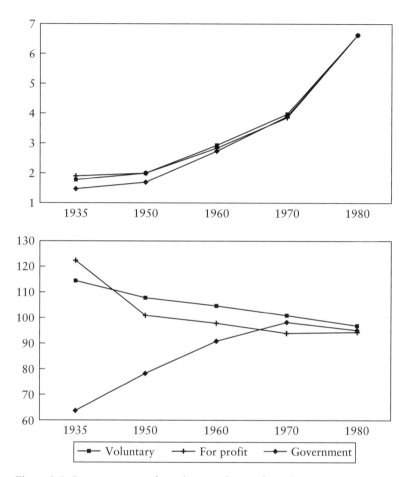

Figure 2.5 Occupancy rates for voluntary, for-profit, and government hospitals by year (actual/normalized)

classified as "significant events" by the Nuclear Regulatory Commission, safety system failures, and radiation exposure. Without exception, the plants that were in 1985 the worst performers on these dimensions improved substantially over time, while the best performers changed little or not at all. Figure 2.6 displays annual numbers of scrams for the best ten and worst ten US nuclear plants, while figure 2.7 shows annual numbers of safety system failures for nuclear plants.[7] The NRC has observed two consequences of this diminution in variance of its key safety indicators. First, correlations among safety measures have declined, and individual measures are now best predicted by their prior

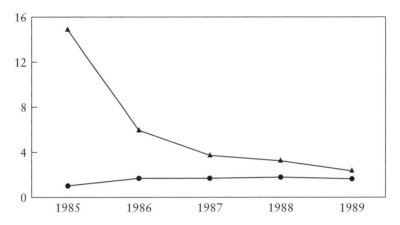

Figure 2.6 Number of scrams for ten best and ten worst nuclear plants

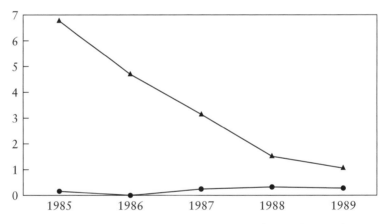

Figure 2.7 Number of safety system actuations for ten best and ten worst nuclear plants

values. Second, there remain few consistent predictors of safety outcomes other than their prior values.

Automotive defects

Variance in the quality of new automobiles sold in the United States has also diminished due to positive learning. Since 1987, J. D. Power and Associates has tracked the number of defects reported by automobile owners during the first ninety days of ownership. In 1987, an average of 166 defects per 100 vehicles were reported, and the gap between the best (Toyota Cressida) and worst (Alfa Romeo Milano) cars was

340 defects per 100 vehicles. By 1997, reported defects had dropped to an average of 81 per 100, and the gap between the best (Lexus LS400) and worst (Pontiac Firebird) cars was only 142 defects. Meanwhile, the quality gap between cars and light trucks has also diminished. From a gap of 40 defects in 1990 (180 defects per 100 light trucks and 140 defects per 100 cars) the quality gap decreased to 11 defects per vehicle in 1997 – 92 defects per 100 trucks compared to 81 defects per 100 cars.[8]

Learning and the search for new measures

Diminished variance in performance measures in spheres as disparate as major league baseball, hospitals, nuclear plants, and automotive quality reflects learning that occurs as organizations observe one another and converge with respect to structure and performance. Social scientists call convergence where similarities have replaced differences *organizational isomorphism.*[9] Normally, such convergence is associated with permanence and stability. Society has converged on ways of doing things, on conventions, on norms. But in the case of performance measures, convergence is a source of impermanence: as the variance of a measure declines, the measure is questioned and new measures are sought. This principle is illustrated most dramatically by gross mortality rates in hospitals, which were introduced by Florence Nightingale in the mid-nineteenth century. Almost as soon as gross mortality rates began to be calculated and compared across hospitals, variance in mortality all but vanished. As Duncan Neuhauser wrote in 1971, "the quality of medical care can be measured if the differences are great enough … The mortality rate after [Nightingale's] arrival was reduced from 42% to 2.2%. This implies that differences between a good and not-so-good hospital in the US today is comparatively small, so Nightingale's gross measure of quality is no longer adequate."[10]

By the same token, J. D. Power's survey of initial car quality is widely considered obsolete.

"The IQS is no longer of value to the customer," Vic Doolan, president of BMW of North America, Inc., said in a recent interview… "You have to credit Power for changing the way the industry thinks, but the usefulness of that stuff is past," said George Peterson, president of the rival consulting firm AutoPacific Group in Santa Ana, Calif., and a former Power analyst. "How can you get any better? The room for product quality improvement is pretty slim."[11]

As a general proposition, convergence of a performance measure triggers a search for alternative measures. For example, diminished variance in its safety measures has caused the Nuclear Regulatory Commission to search continually for new measures.[12] The convergence of functional performance measures has been followed by the reemergence of patient mortality as a performance measure for hospitals, but the new mortality measures are procedure-specific rather than hospital-wide. The convergence of the J. D. Power's Initial Quality, which has been the principal measure of automotive quality for the last decade, has led to calls for its replacement.

Perverse learning

Perverse learning – learning that is perverse in the sense that the wrong lessons are learned – can also diminish variance in measured performance outcomes. Perverse learning takes place when diminished variance surrounding a constant or increasing mean occurs without effect on and perhaps to the detriment of actual performance outcomes. Illustrations of perverse learning abound. Teachers teach to test, which is aimed at improving performance in the lower tail of this distribution. The commercial test-preparation industry does this unabashedly – the goal is to insure that clients' test scores are high enough to be competitive candidates for admission.[13] Police investigators elicit multiple confessions from suspects in order to maintain clearance rates, which may bear little relation to the actual number of crimes solved.[14] In business, short-term earnings and return-on-investment (ROI) targets in business can also give rise to perverse learning. Managers forced to meet earnings and ROI targets will sometimes meet them by deferring expenses, booking revenues not yet earned, and deferring depreciation actually incurred. In each of these instances, measured performance improves and the variance of measured performance declines, leaving actual performance no better and often worse.

Two cases, one classic and one current, illustrate how measurement potentially or actually triggers perverse learning. The classic case involves the performance of interviewers in a public employment agency in the late 1940s:

> The distorting influence of the measuring instrument is a serious problem in social research. In this bureaucracy, the collection of data on operations, such as the number of interviews each official held, also influenced

the interviewer's conduct. The knowledge that his superior would learn how many clients he had interviewed and would evaluate him accordingly induced him to work faster... this direct effect constituted the major function of performance records for bureaucratic operations... dysfunction results from the fact that indices are not perfectly related to the phenomena they purport to measure. Since interviewers were interested in maximizing their "figures," they tried to do so by various means. Occasionally, a client who had been temporarily laid off expected to return to his former job within the next few days. After confirming this with the employer, the interviewer made out a job order and referred the client to this job. In this way he improved his number of referrals and of placements (and the corresponding proportional indices) without having accomplished the objective these indices were designed to measure, that is, without having found a job for the client.[15]

As this passage illustrates, both positive learning (working faster) and perverse learning (placing workers in jobs from which they had been laid off temporarily) can be triggered by the same performance measure. This is not unusual: the effects of positive and perverse learning often cannot be separated, and a manager does not know how much of the improvement in a measure reflects actual improvement. All managers do know is that measured performance has improved while its variability has diminished.

The contemporary case involves alleged grade inflation at Harvard. In the spring of 2001, the dean of Harvard College reported that 49 percent of undergraduate grades were As, up from 23 percent in 1986, triggering a wide-ranging debate on grade inflation. Some viewed the doubling of A grades as positive and reflecting improved performance since Harvard College students are brighter (as measured by SAT scores, but see below on the commercial test-preparation industry) and harderworking than ever. But some perceived that professors have learned that giving poor grades can be costly. One cost is internal ("There's a feeling that you shouldn't pass judgment in a way that might hurt someone's self-esteem," according to Professor Harvey Mansfield). Another is exposure to relentless student pressure (a *Boston Globe* reporter wrote, "While badgering a professor for a higher grade was once considered audacious, many students paying tens of thousands of dollars in tuition today feel a right to lobby for a higher grade..."[16]).

A key question, of course, is whether higher grades or compression of grades is the problem. *New York Times* education columnist Richard

Rothstein argues that the problem is compression, that is invariance rather than inflation:

...rising grades pose a problem that rising prices do not. Prices can rise without limit, but grades cannot go above A+. When more students get A's, grades no longer show which ones are doing truly superior work. This is called "grade compression" and is probably a more serious problem than grade inflation.

Students at Harvard who easily get A's may be smarter, but with so many of them, professors can no longer reward the very best with higher grades. Losing this motivational tool could, paradoxically, cause achievement to fall.[17]

This analysis is helpful as far as it goes. But it could go further. As will be seen, firms can and do change performance measures when existing measures lose variance, but schools have few alternatives to letter grades so long as they wish to maintain comparability of grades across courses and disciplines – in other words, so long as they wish to roll up grades in individual courses into an overall grade point average. More nuanced appraisals of academic performance would be less likely to suffer compression at the upper tail but would lose comparability and hence roll-up capability. Forced grade distributions would avoid grade compression while retaining comparability and roll-up capability, but they would most likely exacerbate competitiveness, discourage students from taking the most challenging classes, and unfairly punish students whose accomplishments are excellent but not exceptional.

Selection

Selection processes can also cause performance measures to run down. Selection is often an outcome of learning, whether positive or perverse, and thus not separable from learning. The running down of batting averages is partly due to selection: as the minor league farm system developed, more proficient selection of both batters and pitchers occurred, yielding convergence in batting averages. Selection operates on firms in much the same way: over time, new entrants are attracted to a market, high performers are retained, and low performers are weeded out. The result, of necessity, is declining variance in performance.

The history of money market mutual funds (MMMFs) from their inception in the mid-1970s to the early 1990s provides a dramatic

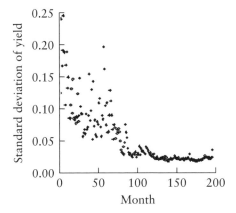

Figure 2.8 Standard deviations of yields, all MMMFs

illustration of how selection causes performance measures to run down. From mid-1975 to late 1991, the number of MMMFs grew from 29 to 543. Many new entrants were attracted, but some MMMFs folded or merged as well. During this interval, the variability of MMMF yields (which are dividends paid to shareholders, since share values are fixed at $1) declined dramatically. Figure 2.8 displays the standard deviations of monthly yields for all MMMFs in existence from September 1975 (month 1 in the figure) through December 1991 (month 196). The pattern of declining variability is unmistakable, especially after 1983. Yields for different types of MMMFs also decline in variability over time. Figure 2.9, for example, displays standard deviations of yields of MMMFs investing in prime corporate debt. The pattern here parallels the declining variability observed for all MMMFs. Figure 2.10 displays standard deviations of yields of MMMFs investing in high yield debt – junk bonds. Here, the variability of yields declines markedly over time, but the pattern of decline is somewhat different: high yield MMMFs do not appear until 1980; the variability of yields of MMMFs investing in junk bonds is somewhat greater than the variability of yields of MMMFs investing in prime corporate debt; and yields of MMMFs investing in junk bonds converge somewhat later than yields of MMMFs investing in prime corporate debt. The experience of high yield in comparison with prime corporate MMMFs suggests that running down occurs more slowly in volatile environments than in stable environments.

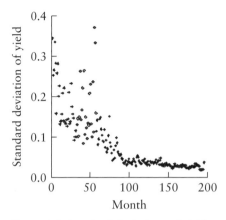

Figure 2.9 Standard deviations of yields, prime corporate MMMFs

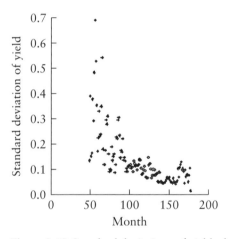

Figure 2.10 Standard deviations of yields, high yield MMMFs

Suppression

Differences in performance are often suppressed, especially when such differences persist. This phenomenon occurs so routinely as to hardly be noticed in personnel matters, where performance ratings creep toward the upper end of whatever scale is used and pay differentials all but vanish despite glaring differences in individual performance.[18] A parallel phenomenon occurs in the assessments of organizational performance. To illustrate: a 1918 survey of hospital quality conducted by the American College of Surgeons found that only 89 of the 692 hospitals with more than 100 beds met minimum ACS standards for patient outcomes. The results were so appalling that all copies of the results were burned and functional performance measures were substituted for patient outcomes in subsequent surveys.[19] Measures showing differences in patient outcomes are still controversial. When statistics on cardiac bypass surgery outcomes for Pennsylvania hospitals and doctors were released in 1992, they were immediately labeled "patently misleading and potentially harmful" by the Pennsylvania Medical Society.[20]

Attempts to suppress intractable performance differences also occur from time to time in schools. To illustrate:

Schools Chancellor Joseph A. Fernandez wants to stop compiling annual rankings of New York City schools by reading levels, probably the most widely used measure for comparing the effectiveness of schools... [Fernandez] said he would seek to abolish the... rankings, which list the city's 633 elementary schools and 179 junior high schools in the order of the overall student achievement on the tests.[21]

Here as elsewhere, the causes of suppression lie in the logic of performance measurement. Performance measurement is useful if it exposes differences between low and high performers and if improvement occurs subsequently – which, as we have seen, diminishes differences and causes new measures to be sought. Where measures expose differences but improvement does not follow, little is to be gained by drawing further attention to differences; and in such situations there is a greater likelihood that differences will be suppressed.

Consensus

Social consensus can also cause performance measures to run down. Consider the market for initial public offerings (IPOs), which behaves quite differently from the larger stock and bond markets because relatively little reliable financial information exists about firms at the time their shares are first offered to the public. IPO prices experience large fluctuations during the first few days of trading and then trade in a narrower range. This is the well known "seasoning effect" for IPOs. The "seasoning effect" is conventionally explained as a function of information. As the market's appraisal of an IPO is revealed over time, it trades in a narrower range. Less well known and less understood than the "seasoning effect" is the effect of a firm's age at the time of issuance of its IPO on the subsequent volatility of IPO prices. The measures conventionally used to gauge the post-issuance volatility of IPOs vary greatly for new firms but are less dispersed for established firms, firms that have been in business many years before offering their shares to the public. Not only do measures of IPO volatility tend to decline with the age of the firm at the time of issuance of the IPO, but this convergence is so marked that the volatility of IPOs of established firms is little different from the volatility of the market as a whole.

The impact of firm age on the volatility of IPOs is shown in figure 2.11. All IPOs valued at $1.5 million or more from July 1977 through December 1984 are included in these figures.[22] Figure 2.11 displays the systematic variance or market beta as a function of firm age over the first 250 trading days following an IPO's issuance, figure 2.12 displays the unsystematic or residual variance as a function of firm age over the first 250 days, and figure 2.13 displays the standard deviation of IPO prices as a function of age over the first 20 days of trading. (Systematic and unsystematic variance are not separated in figure 2.13). Figure 2.11 shows that market betas converge toward unity as firm age at the time of the IPO increases – in other words, the older the

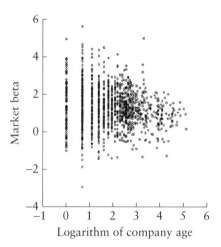

Figure 2.11 Market betas by logarithm of company age for IPOs, July 1977–December 1984

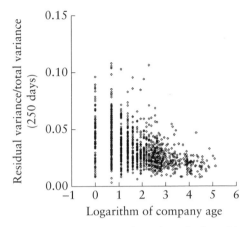

Figure 2.12 Unsystematic variance by logarithm of company age for IPOs, July 1977–December 1984

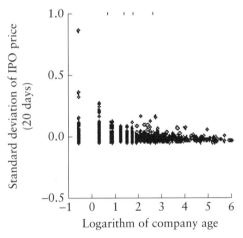

Figure 2.13 Twenty-day total variance by logarithm of company age for IPOs, July 1977–December 1984

firm, the more the volatility of the IPO reflects volatility in the market as a whole. Figure 2.12 shows that unsystematic variance over the first 250 trading days decreases sharply with firm age at the time of the IPO, and figure 2.13 shows that total variance over the first 20 days decreases sharply with firm age. These results, importantly, hold in regression models where firm size, size of the IPO, and size of the industry are controlled. Indeed, firm age at the time of issuance of the IPO is by far the strongest predictor of systematic variance and unsystematic variance over the first 250 trading days and of total variance over the first 20 trading days.

One interpretation of these results is that age is a surrogate for what is already known about a firm. Thus, the older the firm, the more that is known about the causes and sustainability of its performance, and hence the smaller the perturbations in its share price as new information or misinformation surfaces. The problem with this interpretation is that there may not be better information about older than newer firms – for example, firms not publicly traded typically do not issue audited financial statements. A different interpretation is that older firms are more widely known than newer firms – more people recognize their existence and share beliefs about them, whether or not these beliefs are founded in fact. In the argot of organizational theory, older firms are more institutionalized than younger firms, and they are more stable in most respects than younger firms as a consequence.[23] The proposition I am suggesting here, then, is as follows: in the absence or near-absence of objective financial information and market analysis, the stronger the social consensus regarding a firm as indexed by its age, and the less volatile its performance as indexed by the temporal volatility of its IPO. Figure 2.11, then, can be read as follows: older firms bringing IPOs to market are better known and better institutionalized than younger firms. As a consequence, the volatility of their shares reflects the volatility of the market – note in figures 2.11 and 2.12 that betas converge toward unity and unsystematic variance moves toward zero with advancing age – and changes in their share prices may reflect more about the market than information revealed about the firm subsequent to the IPO. I am not dismissing market measures of risk as unimportant, but I am suggesting that if a firm has survived long enough, a social consensus formed prior to the IPO will cause the volatility of its shares, though newly listed, to reflect mainly the volatility of the market.

External change and the running down of performance measures

Although performance measures frequently decline in variability over time, external conditions can induce variability into performance measures that might otherwise converge. Commercial banks are a case in point. Massive regulatory changes in the late 1970s and early 1980s (which, among other things, placed commercial banks in competition with S&Ls) coupled with upward shifts in interest rates created opportunities for some banks but difficulties for others, disadvantaging mainly smaller banks. Figure 2.14 displays series for return on total assets for US commercial banks from 1968 through 1982, the only years for which such data are available consistently. ROA is displayed for banks of different size ranges, under $5 million in assets, assets between $5 and $10 million, $10 to $25 million, $25 to $100 million, and over $100 million. Some shifting of banks between categories occurred as their assets grew, so the data are not strictly comparable over time. Even so, these series show that performance differences across banks of different sizes increased substantially over time, and markedly so toward the end of the series. The same pattern, it should be noted, holds for return on equity and other indicators of bank financial performance. Running down is not evident – quite the opposite occurs, in fact. The same pattern, it should be noted, holds for two other bank performance measures not displayed, rate of return on loans and the ratio of wages to assets.

In examining these series, it is useful to keep in mind changes in interest rates occurring in the 1968–82 interval. The prime rate lending charged to the most creditworthy customers had remained at about 4.5 percent through 1965 but moved above 8 percent toward the end of 1969 before declining somewhat. A second spike in the prime rate occurred in 1974, when it approached 11 percent. And from 1980 through 1982, the prime rate reached unprecedented levels, staying above 15 percent through much of this interval and peaking, in 1981, at 19 percent. Looking across the series in figure 2.14, it is clear that the performance measures diverged noticeably when interest rates peaked first in 1974 and when rates rose dramatically from 1980 through 1982. It is also clear that the regulatory changes of the early 1980s were very much to the disadvantage of small banks.

These results carry an interesting, indeed a paradoxical implication. In stable environments, performance measures run down and hence lose some if not all of their capacity to discriminate good from bad performance. Running down can be caused by several forces – positive learning, perverse learning, selection, suppression, and consensus – and it can be very difficult to distinguish these causes. Running down

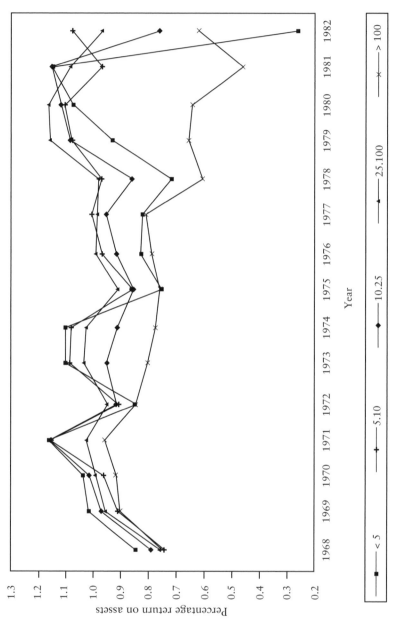

Figure 2.14 Return on assets for commercial banks (classified by assets in millions of dollars)

is, apparently, attenuated by turbulence in the environment. But turbulence in the environment makes measurement noisy in the sense that it diminishes our ability to project from the present to the future and hence our confidence that any measure contains meaningful information about the economic performance of the firm, which lies ahead. Not only, then, is there the "use-it-and-lose-it" principle in performance measurement, but there is the obverse risk that measures that have retained their variability due to environmental turbulence will lose their capacity to anticipate future economic results due to this turbulence.

Changing measures

When existing measures run down, will organizations seek new performance measures that differ slightly or sharply from existing ones? A simple thought experiment yields a counterintuitive result. On the one hand, when existing measures have run down, the new measures sought will not be sharply different from existing measures. Businesses will not replace financial measures with measures of social performance, and professors will not replace measures of research productivity with measures of student contact hours. On the other hand, new measures that are strongly correlated with existing measures will not be sought either, because such measures would be redundant and would simply substitute one set of measures that have run down for another. Fahrenheit and centigrade temperature scales, for instance, contain identical information. Thus, if an existing measure has run down, any new measure strongly correlated with that measure will also have run down. The likelihood, then, is that new measures will be weakly correlated or uncorrelated but not negatively correlated with measures that have run down. In other words, the new measures that will be sought when existing measures have run down will be different from but not antagonistic to existing measures.

The case of General Electric

The experience of General Electric illustrates the tendency of firms to seek new measures different from but not antagonistic to existing measures. Since the 1950s, GE has changed its performance measures several times, oscillating between simple and well-defined measures and complicated and in some instances ill-defined measures. Before

GE was decentralized in the early 1950s, planning and budgeting were centralized in the upper echelons of the company, and the performance of operating units was assessed largely against budgetary targets. Once a fully divisionalized organizational structure was in place, centralized planning and budgeting no longer made sense. It seemed appropriate to develop a set of measures that would permit business unit managers to assess past accomplishments and project future performance.

GE's "Measurements Project," initiated in 1951, was intended to develop performance metrics that could be applied on a decentralized basis. The Measurements Project had three subprojects: operational measurement, functional measurements, and measurements of the work of managing. Eight categories of operational measures emerged over time: profitability, market position, productivity, product leadership, personnel development, employee attitudes, public responsibility, and balance between short-range and long-range goals.

Primary and secondary measures were sought for each class of operational measures. For example, profitability measures included residual dollar profit (basically, profits less the cost of capital, much like today's EVA) and the ratio of residual profits to value added (sales minus materials and parts costs). Measures of market position included share of markets now served as well as share of potential markets. Productivity measures, interestingly, were never decided by the staff of the Measurements Project during its twenty years of existence. These measures encountered some resistance at first, particularly from the comptroller's staff, but they gradually took hold as the middle-management ranks of GE swelled. Not only were the new performance measures dramatically different from the budgetary targets used previously without being antagonistic to these targets, but they were also very different from each other.[24] The Measurements Project wound down in the early 1970s before its work was completed. A definitive set of metrics for General Electric was never established, in all likelihood because at GE as elsewhere no metrics are definitive for long.

General Electric's performance measures shifted dramatically in the late 1970s when Jack Welch became GE's chairman. Welch perceived that the company's existence was imperiled and embarked on a program of weeding out inefficient business units. The selection criteria were of the utmost simplicity and severity: units not either first or second in profitability and growth in their respective industries would be either sold or shut. This policy was pursued for nearly thirteen years – one should keep in mind that the measures produced by the Measurements Project had been in place for nearly three decades before they were changed – during which time Mr. Welch earned the nickname "Neutron Jack" for firing people while the buildings remained standing. The company's profitability grew substantially during this period while its employee roster shrunk.

But as General Electric has prospered, its attention has also shifted to new ventures and markets, especially in Asia, and there has been gradual recognition of limits to continual rationalization of the company. Of particular concern is the adverse impact on employee commitment and initiative, both recognized as essential to any fast-moving global enterprise. For this reason and for other reasons as well, new and very different values for General Electric were announced by Mr. Welch in 1992:

Mr. Welch exemplified the relentless executive willing to mow down any employees standing between him and a brighter bottom line. Through layoffs, plant closings, and the sale of businesses, he eliminated 100,000 jobs, leaving 284,000. As his company's profits increased, his style was widely respected and imitated.

Now Mr. Welch has arrived at a "set of values we believe we will need to take this company forward, rapidly, through the 1990s and beyond." Trust and respect between workers and managers is essential, he said. Managers must be "open to ideas from anywhere."

In Mr. Welch's view, the sort of manager who meets numerical goals but has old-fashioned attitudes is the major obstacle to carrying out these concepts. "This is the individual who typically forces performance out of people rather than inspires it: the autocrat, the big shot, the tyrant," he said.

Still, tyrants will get a taste of Jack Welch's older motivational techniques.

They will adapt, or GE will "part company with them if they cannot."[25] General Electric's "work-out" program, a policy requiring managers to respond to suggestions from their staff, and 360-degree evaluation of managers followed from the values of empowerment, boundarylessness, and openness to new ideas.

Yet another chapter in the saga of performance measurement at GE unfolded in the late 1990s. While not renouncing empowerment, boundarylessness, and openness, CEO Jack Welch determined that quality control is now the company's number one priority, a matter of survival. GE's quality program . . . involves training "Black Belts" for four months in statistical and other quality-enhancing measures. The

Black Belts then spend all their time roaming GE plants and setting up quality improvement projects. Welch has "told young managers that they haven't much future at GE unless they are selected to become Black Belts. The company has trained 2,000 of them and plans to increase that number to 4,000 by year end and to 10,000 by year 2000."[26] For more senior managers, there is a different incentive for implementing the quality control program. Forty percent of their bonuses depend on successful implementation of it.

General Electric's experience since the 1950s suggests several patterns. First, dramatic changes in performance measures do occur in stellar firms like GE, suggesting that performance measures tend to exhaust themselves as strategies succeed. New performance measures, moreover, tend to be very different from existing measures, although rarely antagonistic to them (note, however, the contrast between the new and the "older motivational technique" above). Changing performance measures thus does not signal failure and may augur well for success. Second, the changes in performance measures at GE were sometimes in the direction of elaboration and sometimes in the direction of consolidation, suggesting that successful firms are attentive to the number of measures they are tracking. In the 1950s and 1960s, the "Measurements Project" elaborated measures. In the 1970s, Jack Welch consolidated measures (first or second – or else). In the early 1990s, Mr. Welch elaborated measures ("work-out"), but in the late 1990s he consolidated measures again (quality control). Third, firms less confident than GE may be less willing to discard spent metrics and, as a consequence, find themselves less able to make strategic choices and focus on a limited set of objectives.

A quantitative test

The proposition that new performance measures tend to be uncorrelated with earlier measures is difficult to prove. A corollary of this proposition can be tested, however. If information is lost as earlier performance measures run down but restored when new performance measures uncorrelated with earlier measures are added, then performance measures used by more successful firms should exhibit somewhat weaker correlations than performance measures used by less successful firms. In fact, one of the PIMS (Profit Impact of Market Strategy) databases shows that the most rapidly growing business units exhibit the weakest corrrelations among measured performance outcomes. Eight performance measures describing some 2700 business units are in the SPI4 data file of the PIMS database.[27] Of the eight measures, three are returns-based, including return on investment, and return on sales, and internal rate of return. Three are non-financial measures: productivity, gauged as change in value added per employee, product quality, which taps change in quality relative to a firm's top three competitors, and image, which is measured as change in comparison with the three largest competitors. Finally, there are two growth measures: growth in sales and growth in market share. Three sets of correlations among these performance measures were computed, one for business units experiencing rapid growth in assets, a second for units whose assets remain essentially flat, and the third for business units with declining assets. These correlations are lowest for businesses whose assets are growing and highest for declining-asset business units. Of the twenty-eight correlations among the eight performance measures, ten are negative for business units whose assets are growing, nine are negative for business units whose assets are flat, but only one is negative for business units whose assets are declining.[28] This pattern holds when other variables, industry and stage of product life cycle are controlled.[29] These data suggest, although they do not necessarily prove, that having performance measures that are different from but not antagonistic to each other – in other words, uncorrelated performance measures – may advantage a firm, or, somewhat differently, that uncorrelated measures do not necessarily disadvantage a firm.

To recapitulate, I suggested that as performance measures run down, new measures uncorrelated with existing measures appear. As we saw earlier, the correlation of batting averages with newer measures of player performance is low; hospitals replaced outcome measures with functional measures but are returning to outcome-based performance measures; J. D. Power is actively considering new measures of automotive quality differing from the number of defects reported in their Initial Quality Survey. Uncorrelated measures may actually advantage firms. The recent history of measurement at General Electric, which has moved from budget-based performance measures prior to the 1950s, to the elaborate performance assessment scheme developed by the "Measurements Project" of the 1960s and 1970s, to Jack Welch's simple but severe regimen of the 1980s, to a corporate philosophy rife with fuzzy concepts requiring multiple measures in the early 1990s, and recently to a new emphasis on quality control, is consistent with this proposition. So are some quantitative results based on the PIMS data showing business units having the lowest correlations among performance measures to have the highest rates of business growth.

There are several ways to interpret these observations. The simplest is that simple and stable performance measures do not lead to business success. More realistically, while small and stable measures may lead to success for small firms in stable environments – keep in mind Envirosystems from chapter 1 – success in large organizations may hinge on having a larger set of measures that are different from but not antagonistic to each other and on replacing measures as they run down.

Can running down be inconsequential?

There are, of course, some circumstances where the variance of a performance measure is unimportant and measures do not change even if they do run down. But these circumstances are unusual. Consider once more the United Way thermometer discussed in chapter 1. Not only is the same thermometer used every year, but the same measure – pledges to date – is used to gauge performance year after year. The simplest explanation for the persistence of pledges to date is that it is known to predict the result sought. A department achieving 50 percent of its target in the first two days of a five-day pledge drive is on target and performing well; a department failing to meet 50 percent of its target is missing the mark. Cross-departmental variation is almost immaterial under the circumstances. What is material is the comparison of each department's pledges to date with its target, from which it is possible to judge performance because the likelihood of meeting the target given current pledges is known from experience.

Relative performance measurement and running down

Now let's alter these circumstances. Imagine extending the United Way drive to a year, or even two years. Lacking experience with an extended drive, coordinators will not know what fraction of pledges at the end of the first week is indicative of being on target, nor will they know whether pledges at the end of the first week bear any relevance to the ultimate outcome of the campaign.

Now imagine an extended United Way drive without a specific target but, rather, a goal of maximizing contributions. Because there is no target, no amount of experience would enable coordinators to judge whether pledges at the end of the first week or at any point in the campaign are on target. Extending the time horizon and substituting maximization for specific targets, then, makes it impossible to judge performance by comparing pledges to date with a target for total pledges. As a consequence, coordinators will begin watching one another and comparing pledges to date. Such comparisons allow coordinators to rate their performance relative to each other, although the conclusions they draw from these ratings may prove misleading because short-term accomplishments may have little bearing on long-term results. Such comparisons, moreover, will cause coordinators to imitate each other's behavior and ultimately to perform similarly, since it is a law of human behavior that people who watch one another will eventually behave like one another.[30] Extending the United Way drive and replacing specific targets with the goal of maximizing pledges, in other words, eventually causes differences in pledges to date to diminish and the measure to run down.

Many performance measures more closely resemble those of a protracted United Way campaign whose objective is to maximize the result than those of a typical one-week United Way campaign with a specific target. In business, as in the protracted United Way drive, performance is measured relative to peers rather than relative to a target – think of any measure used to benchmark firms against one another. The relationship of performance measures to the result sought is uncertain because the result lies far ahead. Performance measures lose variance over time because people who watch one another in order to appraise their performance also learn from one another. The impact of batting averages on team standings is uncertain since success at bat does not always translate into runs and wins, baseball players nonetheless strive to improve their batting averages, and the combined forces of learning and selection produce better batters (and better pitchers as well) whose batting averages have become nearly indistinguishable and hence of little consequence for the game. Automotive quality measured by initial defects, similarly, is judged against the competition. The impact of numbers of initial defects on sales and profits is uncertain because many other factors influence sales and profits, automobile manufacturers nonetheless strive to reduce defects, and the combined forces of learning and selection also produce cars that are so nearly defect-free in the first 90 days that initial defects have become of little consequence for sales and profits.

The use-it-and-lose-it principle in performance measurement

There are many lessons for managers. The most important is this: the use-it-and-lose-it principle operates in performance measurement. Measures that initially discriminate, or appear to discriminate, good from bad performance lose the capacity to discriminate as their variability declines and they run down. Measures run down for several reasons, including positive learning, perverse learning or gaming, selection of people or organizations with superior performance attributes, suppression of measures that fail to show improvement, and social consensus.

Running down is caused by people's behavior when they are exposed to performance measures. Often, however, it is difficult to pinpoint which kind of behavior causes measures to run down – specifically, positive learning or less desirable behavior – and for this reason measures that have run down must be replaced by measures that have not. New measures with variability, in particular, must be different from run-down measures having little variability. Thus, slugging percentage replaces batting average, functional measures of hospital performance replace gross mortality, new-car defects weighted by severity replace unweighted defects.

A secondary lesson is that running down is attenuated by turbulence in the environment. But turbulence, in turn, erodes the capacity of any measure to anticipate future cash flows, which comprise the economic performance of the firm.

The running down of performance measures forces changes in some measures and leaves the remainder largely uncorrelated with the new measures, creating some ambiguity as to how performance should be measured. This ambiguity is at the core of the performance measurement enterprise. One way of addressing this ambiguity is to make a virtue of necessity and treat the performance of the firm as if it were multidimensional because our performance measures happen multidimensionally. Multidimensionality is the essence of the balanced scorecard. The problem is that treating performance as multidimensional makes it very difficult to appraise the overall performance of the firm or to compensate people for their performance. The next chapter, which concerns the "balanced scorecard," focuses on the problem of combining diverse performance measures into a single appraisal of performance.

The bottom line

- An important test of any performance measure is its ability to discriminate good from bad performance. In other words, the measure must reveal differences in performance.
- Many, although not all, performance measures lose the capacity to discriminate good from bad performance with use. This is the running down of performance measures.
- There are several causes of running down, among them positive learning, perverse learning (gaming), selection, suppression, and social consensus. Since it is difficult to distinguish improvement from other causes of running down, all measures that have run down are suspect.
- Turbulent environments attenuate the running down of performance measures. But, paradoxically, such turbulence makes it less certain that measures will contain information about the economic performance of the firm, which lies ahead.
- Firms seek new and different measures to replace measures that have run down. Since new measures strongly correlated with measures that have run down will themselves have run down, the new measures will be weakly correlated with existing measures. Performance measures thus may be uncorrelated for good reason.

Appendix: Correlations among performance measures

	ROS	IRR	PROD	QUAL	IMAG	SALE	SHARE
High asset growth business units only (N = 548)							
ROI	0.811	0.517	0.124	−0.137	−0.057	0.056	−0.124
IRR	—	—	0.033	0.057	0.110	0.415	0.148
PROD	—	—	—	0.032	−0.024	−0.050	−0.022
QUAL	—	—	—	—	0.413	0.171	0.171
IMAG	—	—	—	—	—	0.194	0.222
SALE	—	—	—	—	—	—	0.498
Constant asset business units only (N = 1648)							
ROI	0.845	0.328	0.290	−0.075	−0.092	0.059	−0.031
ROS	—	0.306	0.269	−0.087	−0.086	0.058	−0.034
IRR	—	—	0.010	0.088	0.049	0.431	0.233
PROD	—	—	—	0.045	−0.092	−0.038	−0.074
QUAL	—	—	—	—	0.348	0.171	0.225
IMAG	—	—	—	—	—	0.136	0.176
SALE	—	—	—	—	—	—	0.529
Declining asset business units only (N = 550)							
ROI	0.872	0.283	0.293	−0.013	0.016	0.201	0.141
ROS	—	0.292	0.287	0.015	0.022	0.241	0.165
IRR	—	—	0.044	0.132	0.131	0.425	0.238
PROD	—	—	—	0.096	−0.116	0.239	0.046
QUAL	—	—	—	—	0.349	0.174	0.185
IMAG	—	—	—	—	—	0.230	0.230
SALE	—	—	—	—	—	—	0.485

3 | *In search of balance*

BALANCED performance measurement is an appealing concept, but in practice it is very difficult. Balanced measurement involves measuring both financial and non-financial performance. Often, non-financial performance is measured in several domains – for example the customer, internal processes, and learning and innovation. The problem posed by balanced measurement is not measuring non-financial performance alongside financial performance; as we saw in chapter 1, most firms do this routinely. The problem, rather, is finding the right non-financial measures and then using these measures in combination with financial measures to appraise and compensate performance.

A balanced set of measures will include non-financial measures that add information about the economic performance of the firm beyond what is contained in financial measures – in other words, non-financial measures that look ahead. But as we saw in chapter 1, finding non-financial measures that actually look ahead, as opposed to measures that plausibly look ahead, can be challenging. Finding a satisfactory way to combine ratings on several measures into an overall appraisal of performance is also challenging. It is easy to rate and rank, and hence appraise and compensate, performance based on a single measure. But it is difficult to combine ratings on several measures into an overall performance rating in a way that does not have pernicious effects.

As early as the 1970s, managers were skeptical that the performance of the firm could be captured by a single financial measure such as earnings per share. But few managers were compensated on both financial and non-financial measures until the 1990s. This reluctance to fold financial and non-financial measures together changed with the publication of two *Harvard Business Review* articles: Robert Eccles' "The performance measurement manifesto" (1991) and Robert Kaplan and David Norton's "The balanced scorecard: measures that drive performance" (1992). The two articles conveyed a similar message:

financial measures alone are insufficient to gauge business performance. Eccles suggested that business models, which are conceptual representations of relationships between non-financial measures and financial results, be used to identify the non-financial drivers of business outcomes. Kaplan and Norton recommended that measurement should take place in the four domains of performance: financial, customer, internal business, and learning and innovation.

Kaplan and Norton's notion of the "balanced scorecard" ultimately proved more influential than Eccles' call for business performance models, although not in the way intended. Kaplan and Norton viewed the "balanced scorecard" primarily as a tool for communicating strategy – in their terms "a framework for action" – and only secondarily as a compensation tool. "The Balanced Scorecard translates an organization's mission into a comprehensive set of performance measures that provides the framework for a strategic measurement and management system."[1] By the mid-1990s, however, between a third and two-thirds of US companies had adopted the balanced scorecard or some variant of it for purposes of appraising and compensating the performance of their managers. Using the balanced scorecard to appraise and compensate performance, it turns out, is more difficult than using the scorecard for strategic measurement. Finding the right scorecard measures – especially non-financial measures that look ahead – is essential both for strategic measurement and for appraising and compensating performance. Combining these measures into an appraisal of overall performance, however, while not essential to strategic measurement, is essential to compensating performance.

From financial measurement to balanced measurement and back again

The difficulty of achieving balanced measurement is well illustrated by intensive analysis of a single case, that of the US retail business of Global Financial Services (GFS) and its Western region in particular. In 1993, GFS shifted from a performance appraisal and compensation system based on a single earnings measure to a balanced-scorecard approach. There were two versions of the "balanced scorecard." Initially, GFS implemented formula-driven compensation in which the weights attached to measures were specified in advance. After two and a half years, formula-driven compensation proved unsatisfactory. It was replaced by a highly subjective system in which the weights attached to individual measures were not fixed in advance but revealed as compensation decisions were made. This subjective compensation system, in turn, encountered considerable resistance from GFS's employees and, ultimately, its senior managers. In 1999, the effort to compensate people on both financial and non-financial performance was scrapped and replaced by a system sensitive only to sales and earnings.

The focus on financial results: business unit earnings and margins

Throughout the 1980s and early 1990s, the principal units of the business were its retail and commercial businesses. All GFS business units were held accountable mainly for financial results. The principal metric was business-unit earnings (essentially revenues less expenditures). The five regional units and more than 400 local branches in the US retail business were responsible for revenues, expenditures, and margins (the difference between revenues and expenditures). However, the substantial costs of operating centralized check-clearing, collection, and data-processing units were not charged to regional units and branch operations. Thus, the margins these units reported were much higher than actual earnings. Bonuses for regional and branch staff were contingent on meeting revenue and margin targets and were calculated as percentages of base salaries. In other words, the compensation system was formulaic.

GFS encountered the shortcomings of financial measurement in the early 1990s when the US real estate market collapsed, leaving the commercial side of the business saddled with several billion dollars of non-performing assets. The initial response was to apply a tourniquet: expenditures and staff were cut dramatically. Once the cash hemorrhage slowed, GFS's management determined that it was critical to measure risks alongside earnings. Specifically, management declared multi-faceted or "textured" performance measurement should replace the exclusive emphasis on financial results. In 1992, the US retail business developed a business model linking non-financial aspects of performance to financial performance. Customer satisfaction was identified as the key driver of profitability and market share and made pivotal to the business model (see figure 3.1). The business model also grouped nineteen activities into five categories of activity driving customer

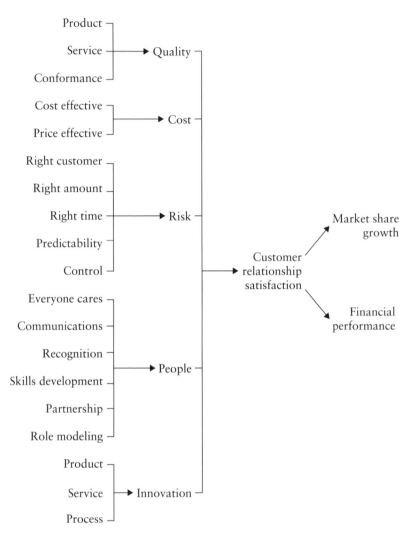

Figure 3.1 1992 business model for GFS US retail operations

satisfaction. The business model did not specify performance measures, nor was the model validated quantitatively. It was strictly a mental model of the business. Even so, the mapping of activities onto desired outcomes conveyed a message that earnings metrics alone could not: that all paths to market share and financial performance led through customer satisfaction.

The "performance improvement program"

In 1993 the business model was translated into a compensation scheme, the "performance improvement program," also known as the "Performance Incentive Plan" (PIP). The purpose of PIP was to promote GFS's strategic mission of being "the best and only place for target customers and businesses to manage all of their money anytime, anywhere, any way they want" and to compensate staff for their accomplishments.

The Performance Incentive Plan was intended to be both balanced and formulaic: it included both financial and non-financial measures, and bonuses were determined by explicit formulas. The measures and formulas used by PIP are summarized in figure 3.1. To receive a quarterly bonus, branches were required to receive satisfactory scores on internal operational audits and to pass a customer-satisfaction hurdle, as measured by a survey of customer satisfaction. The customer-satisfaction measures, like the PIP compensation formulas, evolved over time. In 1993 and 1994, a single question asked customers to rate their overall satisfaction with their primary branch on a seven-point scale. For each branch, the percentage of customers answering in the top two categories, very satisfied and satisfied, was calculated. In 1993, branches with customer-satisfaction levels in the top 75 percent received passing scores. In 1994, customer satisfaction levels statistically equal to or greater than the regional means received passing scores. In 1995, the single question was replaced by a branch quality index, a composite of twenty items believed to have better psychometric properties.[2] Branch-quality indices that were statistically equal to or greater than the regional mean received passing scores in the 1995 version of PIP.

In 1993, branches that passed the customer-satisfaction hurdle received quarterly bonuses for meeting targets in any one of the performance objectives related to growing the business, resource management, and "overall performance." In 1994, branches were also required to meet at least four of the eight performance objectives to be eligible to receive a quarterly bonus. In 1995, the objectives shifted again: to be eligible for bonuses, branches had to pass the branch-quality and audit-score hurdles and meet their financial (revenue and margin) targets as well.

In sum, new hurdles and goals were added to PIP each year. The document outlining each year's program grew accordingly from nine pages in 1993 to seventy-eight pages in 1995. The growing complexity of the PIP formulas had two causes. The first was management's frustration with a formula-driven compensation system that allowed branches to earn bonuses without delivering financial results – in other words, management's belief that PIP was being gamed. Thus, the 1995 PIP program added a financial hurdle that made it much more difficult for unprofitable branches to receive bonuses. The second cause was management's belief that retail banking customers were ultimately clients of GFS, rather than a particular branch, and that their overall satisfaction *with* GFS was more significant for long-term business results than their satisfaction with their branches. As a senior GFS officer stated in 1994, "If we take a focus that 'everything is all right with my area but there's something else wrong out there which is not my concern,' we will lose long term. You own the customer. That's the fundamental building block we have." Thus, overall satisfaction with GFS was added as a performance objective in 1995 – at the same time that the 20-item branch-quality hurdle replaced the single-item branch-satisfaction hurdle. The available data do not permit an objective assessment, but PIP's demise in 1995 suggests that GFS management judged its overall results unsatisfactory.

The balanced scorecard

In early 1995, GFS refined its corporate strategy to focus on five "imperatives" for success over time: achieving good financial results, delivering for customers, managing costs strategically, managing risk, and having the right people in the right jobs. To evaluate progress against these imperatives, each of GFS's principal businesses was required to develop a "balanced scorecard" of related measures. A senior executive outlined the goals of the balanced-scorecard approach in GFS's employee newsletter:

The Balanced Scorecard is a simple matrix that leads us to examine how each business, as well as the whole, does in all of those performance blocks. In the process, we can also assess individual performance against the same criteria. It not only sums up what we want to do, it does it in a way that assures everyone in the company knows what we are trying to accomplish and what is important in getting the job done.

Perhaps the most important thing about how it works is the balance. Our past problems can almost always be traced to too much of a single-minded focus on bottom-line earnings, or building revenues, or something else to the exclusion of other important issues. By forcing us to focus on all of the key performance factors, the Balanced Scorecard keeps us in balance.

The Western region of GFS's US retail business replaced PIP with the balanced scorecard performance evaluation and compensation system in May 1995, and other regions followed in January 1996.

Six categories of performance made up the scorecard: financial performance, strategy implementation, customer performance, control, people-related performance, and standards. The first three scorecard categories were measured using multiple *quantitative* indicators. *Financial performance* was measured by revenues, expenses, and margins. *Strategy implementation* was measured by the number of premier, retail, and business/professional households, household attrition, assets under management, and assets per household through the first quarter of 1996.[3] After that, the strategy measures were retail asset balances, market share, and new households and net revenue per household for each customer category (premier,[4] retail, and business/professional) replacing household attrition, assets under management, and assets per household. *Customer performance* was measured by overall satisfaction with GFS and the branch quality index, both carried over from the 1995 PIP program.

The remaining categories were measured by *qualitative* indicators. *Control* was assessed by the results of periodic internal audits of operations, regulatory compliance, and the integrity of business results reviews. *People-related performance* was judged by performance management, teamwork, training and development, and employee satisfaction.[5] *Standards* were judged by leadership, business ethics and integrity, customer interaction and focus, community involvement, and contribution to the overall business.

Unlike the formula-driven PIP, the balanced scorecard required area directors supervising branch managers to weight various performance measures *subjectively*. First, performance was compared with targets for each of the financial, strategy implementation, and customer measures, resulting in a "par rating" for each measure. ("Below par," "at par," and "above par" signified performance relative to targets.) Ratings on individual measures were then combined subjectively into

	BELOW PAR	PAR	ABOVE PAR	RESULTS	GOAL
FINANCIAL					
Revenues					
Expenses					
Margins					
STRATEGY IMPLEMENTATION					
Premier households					
Retail households					
Business/professional households					
Total households					
New premier households					
New retail households					
New business/professional households					
Total new households					
Lost premier households					
Lost retail households					
Lost business/professional households					
Total lost households					
Cross-sell/split/mergers households					
Premier CNR/HH					
Retail CNR/HH					
Business and professional CNR/HH					
Retail asset balances					
Remote transactions/total transactions					
Market share					
CUSTOMER SATISFACTION					
Overall GFS satisfaction					
Branch quality					
CONTROL					
Audit					
Regulatory					
Business results review					
PEOPLE					
Performance management					
Teamwork					
Training/development – self					
Training/development – others					
Employee satisfaction					
STANDARDS					
Leadership					
Business ethics/integrity					
Customer interaction/focus					
Community involvement					
Contribution to overall business					
OVERALL EVALUATION					

Figure 3.2 Balanced scorecard for GFS US retail operations, 1996

par ratings for the financial, strategy, and customer categories. For the control, people, and standards categories, par ratings for individual criteria were determined subjectively.[6] Finally, an overall performance rating of "below par," "at par," or "above par" was determined subjectively based on par ratings in the six scorecard categories. A similar process was used to appraise the performance of lower-level branch employees. The branch-manager scorecard used by GFS's US retail operations in 1996 is shown in figure 3.2.

Area directors also recommended quarterly bonuses based on overall par ratings of branch managers. Overall par ratings and bonus recommendations were discussed at meetings of the head of the region, his staff (the finance director, human resource director, compensation manager, and service quality director), and all Western region area directors. Discussions typically focused on the justification for the overall rating recommended for the branch manager, particularly above-par ratings making managers eligible for substantial bonuses. The tenor of these discussions shifted from quarter to quarter in response to GFS's shifting priorities. Sometimes, at-par financial performance disqualified a manager from an above-par overall rating. A below-par rating on customer performance could also preclude an above-par overall rating regardless of financial performance. A below-par evaluation on control, which meant that a branch had failed an audit, always precluded an above-par overall evaluation.

Quarterly bonuses were intended to achieve *total* market-based compensation levels (salary plus bonus) appropriate for a branch manager's labor grade and performance level. For example, assume that total compensation for branch managers in the highest of the three labor grades is targeted at *up to* $75,000 annually if performance is at par, *up to* $90,000 if performance is above par, and *up to* $105,000 (or more) if performance is exceptional. If a manager in this labor grade earned a salary of $80,000 and had an above-par performance rating, the *maximum* quarterly bonus would be $2,500 ($10,000/4). If the manager's salary were $90,000 or more, no bonus would be awarded despite the above-par performance. The PIP formula, by contrast, awarded a bonus percentage regardless of base salary (e.g., a branch manager earning $80,000 and eligible for a 15 percent bonus would receive a $3,000 quarterly bonus; at a salary of $90,000 the same person would receive $3,375).

Almost from the outset, the balanced scorecard encountered three kinds of problems. First, the process proved to be extremely complex and time consuming, at least initially. Some area directors spent as much as ten to twelve days per quarter completing scorecards, reviewing them with branch managers, and defending their recommendations. Eighteen months into the process, area directors in the Western region still spent an average of six days per quarter on scorecard issues. Said one, "We dread it every time." Second, branch managers and their employees could not understand how they were compensated. Third, branch managers complained that their evaluations and compensation were tied to measures they could not control. They particularly objected to the measure asking customers to rate their overall satisfaction with GFS. Branch managers felt that they were unfairly held accountable for the centralized check-clearing, collection, credit-card, and data-processing units whose actions they could not control. One Western region branch manager put it this way: "Branch managers are held accountable for all of [GFS], while other managers are not accountable at all under the scorecard. It is an incredible burden to accept full responsibility for [GFS]."

By late 1997, internal resistance forced management to begin rethinking the performance evaluation and compensation system. GFS was publicly committed to a balanced scorecard, but not to any particular implementation of it. The company needed a compensation system that avoided the pitfalls of both PIP and the balanced scorecard. Management believed that PIP failed because it had been gamed: PIP allowed people to earn substantial bonuses by satisfying customers and building the business without delivering bottom-line results. Moreover, efforts to stem gaming by adding new and higher hurdles had only made matters worse. Management did not have a comparable analysis of the failings of the balanced scorecard but knew that a simpler compensation system was needed. By the time a simpler scorecard was ready to be implemented in early 1999, however, new management had taken control of GFS's US retail operations and replaced the balanced scorecard with a sales-based compensation system.

An analysis of the balanced scorecard

The balanced scorecard implemented by GFS was both a set of measures and a way of combining these measures into an appraisal of people's overall performance. The problems GFS encountered with the balanced scorecard and with PIP were due partly to the choice of measures and partly to the way measures were combined. Choosing measures and combining measures are, of course, related problems: the more measures chosen, the more difficult it is to combine them. Kaplan and Norton's formulation of the balanced scorecard provided no guidance about combining measures because the scorecard was intended to communicate strategy rather than to measure and compensate

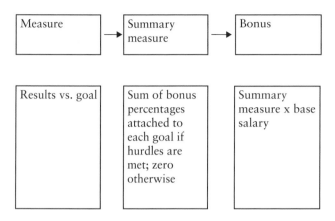

Measured performance *determines* bonus

Figure 3.3 Flowchart of PIP

performance. GFS also focused exclusively on the choice of measures –
at least initially.

Flowcharting the scorecard process

GFS's scorecard process was much more complicated than the process
that had operated under PIP. PIP was formula-driven. Once quarterly
results were assembled, branch manager bonuses followed automatically, as did the bonus pool awarded to branch employees, which, as
a percentage of base salaries, was one-half of the branch manager's
bonus.[7] The mapping of performance onto compensation under PIP
is shown in figure 3.3. There were three steps in the process. Results
were compared to goals, a percentage of base salary was awarded for
each goal attained provided hurdles were met, and the bonus function
was the sum of these percentages multiplied by base salary. The process remained unchanged from 1993 to 1995, even though additional
hurdles and goals were added to the PIP formulas each year.

The five-step scorecard process is illustrated in figure 3.4. The first
step compared results to goals for the financial, strategy-imple-
mentation, and customer-performance categories. The second step appraised each measured result *subjectively* by assigning a par rating
to it, and, in the control, people-related performance and standards
categories, by assigning par ratings to each qualitative performance
standard indicated on the scorecard. In the third step of the process,

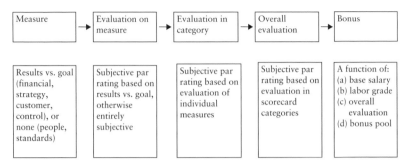

Subjective at three intermediate steps – measured performance *does not* determine compensation

Figure 3.4 Flowchart of balanced scorecard

performance within each of the six scorecard categories was evaluated *subjectively* based on par ratings of individual measures and standards. The fourth step appraised overall performance *subjectively* based on par ratings in the six scorecard categories. The fifth step awarded quarterly bonuses as a function of the employee's base salary, labor market grade, and overall par rating. Individual bonus awards were also affected by the size of the bonus pool and the number of above-par ratings – if the bonus pool was unusually small or if the percentage of above-par ratings was unusually high, then individual awards could be scaled back somewhat.

Given its complexity, it was inevitable that the scorecard process would be perceived as complicated and time consuming. The path from measured performance to bonus awards involved five steps, including three subjective judgments and a bonus calculation driven by three and possibly four factors. The contrast with PIP may have magnified the perceived complexity and time requirements of the scorecard. PIP was Spartan in its simplicity: three steps, all formula-driven. The simplicity of PIP, however, compromised bottom-line performance. The balanced scorecard avoided this outcome but incurred other costs.

Weighting measures

Under PIP, weights attached to individual measures (see table 3.1) were explicit and fixed in advance. Under the balanced scorecard, by contrast, no explicit weights were attached to individual measures. Nor was there a formula for rolling up results on the par scores in the

Table 3.1 *Evolution of the PIP system, 1993–1995*

Year	Hurdles	Performance objectives	Bonus for meeting performance targets (% of base salary)	Additional bonus for extraordinary performance	Additional bonus payments/conditions
1993	Satisfaction with primary branch office – top 75% in region	Margin growth	3%	–	None
		Tier I and II household growth	2%	–	
		Consumer checking balance growth	2%	–	
		B&P checking balance growth	2%	–	
		Revenue growth	2%	–	
		Liability relationship growth	2%	–	
		Expense control	1%	–	
1994	Satisfaction with primary branch office – statistically at or above the regional mean	Margin growth	3%	Up to 1.5%	Bonus payment augmented by multiplier of 10% for satisfaction with primary branch statistically above the regional mean
		Tier I and II household growth	1.5%	Up to 2.5%	
	Operations control – audit score of "A" or "B"	Consumer checking balance growth	1.5%	Up to 2.5%	
		B&P checking balance growth	1.5%	Up to 2.5%	
		Revenue growth	3%	Up to 4.5%	

Table 3.1 *Evolution of the PIP system, 1993–1995 (Continued):*

Year	Hurdles	Performance objectives	Bonus for meeting performance targets (% of base salary)	Additional bonus for extraordinary performance	Additional bonus payments/conditions
		Liability relationship growth	1.5%	Up to 2.5%	
		Expenses/revenues	0.5%	Up to 1%	
		Footings/tier I and II households	0.5%	Up to 1%	
1995	Branch quality index – at or above the regional mean	Overall GFS satisfaction 80%	5%	–	Bonus increased by to 10% for high 2 utilization of remote channels
	Operations control – audit score of "A" or "B"	Target household	2% for growth	Up to 1%	
		Total checking balance	1% for growth	0.5%	
			1% for goal	Up to 0.5%	
	Earn minimum 9 payout for meeting or exceeding revenue/margin growth/goal targets	Liability relationship/ asset revenue margin	1% for growth	Up to 0.5%	
			1% for goal	Up to 0.5%	
			2% for growth[a]	Up to 0.5%	
			2% for goal[a]	Up to 0.5%	
			2.5% for growth[a]	Up to 1%	
			2.5% for goal[a]	Up to 8%	

Note: Bonus percentages apply to branch manager base salaries.
[a] These higher percentages were awarded for extraordinary performance.

six scorecard categories into an evaluation of overall performance or actual quarterly bonus payouts. Instead, weights were attached to measures and par scores in the six categories only implicitly during performance evaluations.

As it turned out, the implicit weights of par ratings in the six scorecard categories varied dramatically from quarter to quarter. The impact of par ratings for financial performance, strategy implementation, customer performance, financial control, people management, and standards on branch managers' overall par ratings varied dramatically throughout the fifteen quarters of the balanced scorecard's implementation in GFS's Western region (the second quarter of 1995 through the fourth quarter of 1998). Eta-squared statistics, which measure the incremental explanatory power of each measure, range from 0.21 to 0.62 for the financial par score, from 0.01 to 0.27 for the strategy par score, from 0.01 to 0.47 for the customer par score, from 0.00 to 0.19 for the control par score, from 0.00 to 0.27 for the people par score, and from 0.00 to 0.25 for the par score for standards over the fifteen quarters of scorecard implementation. The median eta-squared statistics over these quarters was 0.41 for the financial par score, 0.11 for the strategy par score, 0.27 for the customer par score (which, in turn, was driven entirely by overall GFS satisfaction and not at all by the branch quality index), and 0.04, 0.07, and 0.02 respectively for the control, people, and standards par scores.

The impact of par ratings in the same six categories on quarterly bonus payouts was smaller, but still varied greatly. Here, the eta-squared statistics range from 0.07 to 0.51 for the financial par score, from 0.01 to 0.24 for the strategy par score, from 0.00 to 0.37 for the customer par score, and were quite small and statistically insignificant in all but a few instances for the control, people, and standards par scores. The median eta-squared statistics over the fifteen quarters was 0.24 for the financial par score, 0.05 for the strategy par score, 0.08 for the customer par score, and 0.05, 0.03, and 0.01 respectively for the control, people, and standards par scores.

The overall picture that emerges is one of considerably variability in the implicit weights attached to different elements of GFS's scorecard and hence substantial uncertainty about the impact of par scores in the six scorecard-category bonus payouts. This said, the impact of the financial par score on overall par ratings and on quarterly bonuses was greater than that of the par scores in the other five categories. The implication should not be missed: since financial performance was rewarded more consistently than performance in other categories while performance in the people, control, and standards categories was rarely if ever rewarded, *the subjectivity of the scorecard process had the unintended consequence of focusing attention on financial performance*. In other words, the balanced scorecard, as implemented at GFS, created both uncertainty (because performance in all six scorecard categories was rewarded inconsistently) and imbalance (because performance in three of the six scorecard categories was rarely rewarded).

The critical question, of course, is whether the level of uncertainty induced by the subjectivity of the scorecard process was desirable. From the perspective of management, some subjectivity was desirable because it precluded the kind of gaming that had been endemic to PIP. Additionally, subjectivity allowed the compensation system to adapt to changing circumstances of the business and individual branches. From the perspective of branch managers and their employees (and virtually all theories of motivation), however, the level of subjectivity created by the scorecard was undesirable because it eroded perceived connections between measured performance (save for financial performance), the evaluation of performance, and compensation for this performance. The tension between these perspectives is understandable, but it was aggravated by the need to combine several dissimilar measures into an appraisal of overall performance and a bonus payout.

This raises the question of whether the balanced scorecard imposes inconsistent requirements when used to appraise and compensate performance. One requirement is measurement of non-financial performance alongside financial performance in the expectation that at least some non-financial measures will contain information about long-term economic performance not contained in financial measures. Of necessity, the more domains of non-financial performance measured, the more dissimilar measures will be. Another requirement is combining dissimilar measures into an appraisal of overall performance. If measures are combined by formula, as under PIP, they will be gamed quickly and become unreliable as people reach for the low-hanging fruit. But if measures are combined subjectively, as under GFS's version of the balanced scorecard, perceived connections between performance and rewards will erode, and motivation will suffer correspondingly. One possibility is that scorecards can be made more parsimonious so that there are fewer dissimilar measures and hence less gaming of them and less subjectivity in combining them – GFS's scorecard did have more measures than the scorecards of other financial service firms.[8] But to make scorecards truly parsimonious, firms must be able to separate the few non-financial measures that contain information about economic performance from the many measures that do not.

Finding measures that look ahead to bottom-line performance

GFS's management implemented the balanced scorecard to compensate people for performance on measures that drive future business results as well as for current business results. Financial performance, as we have seen, was weighted more consistently and heavily in compensation decisions than performance in other scorecard categories. This raised the question of whether any of the non-financial measures on the scorecard, especially items that were measured objectively, contained information about future financial performance. The analysis modeled changes in branch margins as a function of earlier changes in six strategy implementation measures (number of customers and customer net revenue for three segments, premier households, retail households, and business/professional relationships, and two customer measures, overall GFS satisfaction and the branch quality index, the latter a composite of twenty questionnaire items covering most aspects of branch service. The results, though straightforward, were surprising: the branch quality index had a powerful impact on revenues and margins[9] as well as on the number of retail and business/professional households.[10] The number of premier and retail households and business/professional relationships, however, had no impact on revenues and margins, while the single-item GFS satisfaction measure had no discernible impact on revenues, margins, or households. Figure 3.5 illustrates these results schematically.

When the branch quality index was examined to determine which of its components actually drove revenues and margins, the outcome was also surprising.[11] It had been anticipated that overall satisfaction with the quality of branch service, a single item that was weighted 45 percent in the branch-quality index, would have the greatest impact on revenues and margins. This expectation was not confirmed. Instead, the item that dominated bottom-line results was: "Please rate the overall quality of the teller who last served you..."[12] The perceived quality of

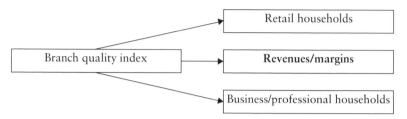

Figure 3.5 Business model of GFS Western region (using branch-quality index)
Note: Questions concerning branch quality asked of retail customers only.

tellers influenced revenues and margins directly, and also indirectly affected revenues and margins through its impact on the perceived overall quality of branch service on the number of retail households served. Perceived quality of branch employees other than tellers (such as investment representatives and branch managers) had no direct impact on revenues and margins, but it influenced bottom-line results indirectly by contributing to the number of business/professional relationships. Interestingly, overall satisfaction with GFS decreased with the number of business/professional relationships (see figure 3.6).[13]

Together, the results shown in figures 3.5 and 3.6 suggest that either the twenty-item branch-quality index or the individual items measuring teller quality, other branch employee quality, and overall branch quality should have entered into branch managers' compensation while overall GFS satisfaction should not have. Whether this conclusion holds going forward is less certain. Figures 3.5 and 3.6, like all empirically grounded business models, describe the past and perhaps the present but not necessarily the future. Teller usage, for example, may decline as retail transactions shift to automated teller machines and internet banking while business/professional and premier customers shift to doing business through personal account representatives. Relationships with GFS units outside of the branch banking system, for example mortgage and credit-card relationships, moreover, may render overall satisfaction with GFS a predictor of revenues and margins outside of branch banking.

Several lessons, then, should be drawn from figure 3.6. First, and most important, it is possible to find non-financial measures predictive of financial performance in firms like GFS and Sears that have three characteristics: (1) they have many business units or branches or outlets; (2) business units perform similar functions; and (3) business units are responsible for financial performance. Second, non-financial measures predictive of financial performance can be used to appraise and compensate performance provided their limitations are understood. These limitations are twofold: (1) predictive measures may not remain predictive as the direction of the business changes or, as suggested in chapter 2, as measures are gamed and they run down; and (2) measures that are not predictive of financial performance may still be predictive if the bottom line is measured incompletely.

There may be a third lesson as well if the results shown in figures 3.5 and 3.6 can be extended beyond GFS: measures that gauge the day-to-day functioning of the organization (such as the quality of the teller who last served you) are more likely to impact the customer than generic measures (such as overall GFS satisfaction). But specific measures of functioning rarely apply across the entire organization and cannot usually be rolled up into a summary measure for the entire organization. The quality of the teller who last served you, for example, has no relevance for customers who never see tellers (an increasing

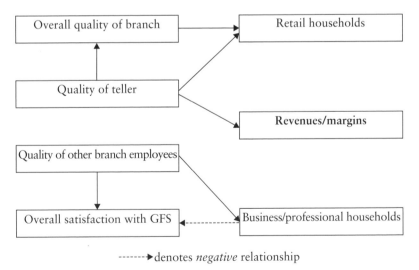

- - - - - ▶ denotes *negative* relationship

Figure 3.6 Business model of GFS Western region (using components of branch-quality index) *Note*: Questions concerning quality and satisfaction asked of retail customers only.

proportion of GFS retail customers) or for GFS customers who do not patronize the retail businesses.

By contrast, generic measures that are removed from the organization's functioning contain less information about bottom-line performance than specific measures of functioning but are easier to roll up from the bottom to the top of the organization. Overall satisfaction with GFS, for example, while easily measured for all of GFS's customers, contains little information about bottom-line performance because customers' points of contact with the organization and their experiences at these sites vary greatly.

The tradeoff is difficult between measures that gauge day-to-day functioning but cannot be rolled up and more generic measures that can be rolled up. Under some circumstances, as we will see in the next two chapters, it is best to avoid this tradeoff by driving bottom-line measures to the level of individual customers and activities performed for them.

What did the balanced scorecard communicate to employees?

Employee surveys taken nine months before and nine months after implementation of the scorecard in the Western region indicate that employees were more likely to agree that "Measures of quality exist to help assess my job performance" after scorecard implementation than before. There was no change in employees' agreement with the statement, "I understand the business goals of [GFS]" between the two surveys, but Western region employees were significantly less likely to agree that "I get adequate information about progress against business goals" after implementation of the scorecard than before it. While the scorecard communicated *measures* more effectively and communicated *strategy* about as effectively as the earlier PIP, it communicated information about *performance* less effectively, probably due to its subjectivity. It appears that the balanced scorecard created uncertainty about compensation. The only evidence on compensation comes from the December 1996 survey of Northern region employees twelve months after the scorecard was rolled out in the region, Fifty-five percent of employees surveyed agreed with the statement, "When it comes to scorecard bonuses, I have no idea who gets what or why."

The elements of balanced performance measurement

At this point, it may be more useful to step back from GFS's implementation of the balanced scorecard to discuss balanced performance measurement more analytically. A framework for this discussion is shown in figure 3.7.

Balanced performance measurement is defined at the apex of figure 3.7. Balanced performance measurement involves measuring, appraising, and compensating both financial and non-financial performance. In principle, balanced measurement does not give priority to some non-financial measures over others, although in practice many firms have focused non-financial measurement in the three categories suggested by Kaplan and Norton – internal process, customer learning, and innovation. Balanced performance measurement, however, does impose two general requirements. The first requirement is finding the right measures, that is financial measures and non-financial measures predictive of long-term financial performance, in other words, non-financial measures that look ahead alongside financial measures that look behind. The second requirement is combining financial and non-financial measures, which are dissimilar, into a single appraisal of performance and a bonus payout or salary increment.

Finding the right measures

Choose the initial measures
The first step toward finding the right measures is initial selection of measures. The initial selection often takes place in the context of a business model or a statement of the firm's strategy. GFS's 1992 business model (see figure 3.1) guided the selection of measures for PIP, and the five strategic "imperatives" GFS announced in 1995 guided the selection of balanced scorecard categories and measures.

Consider tradeoffs between generic and specific measures
The second step is considering tradeoffs between generic measures several steps removed from the functioning of the organization, for example overall GFS satisfaction, and specific measures capturing day-to-day functioning, for example teller quality. Several tradeoffs must be considered. Generic measures apply across the organization, whereas specific measures apply to particular businesses or functions within the

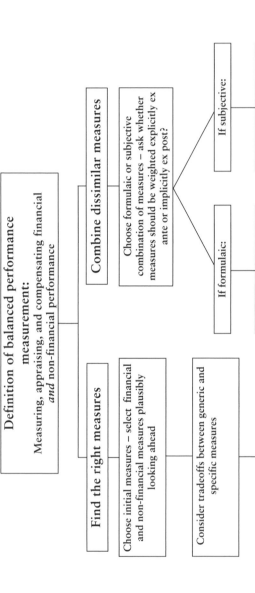

Figure 3.7 The elements of balance

organization. Generic measures usually originate at the top of the organization and are cascaded from top to bottom of the organization, whereas specific measures usually originate at the bottom and cannot be rolled up from bottom to top. Generic measures, additionally, are less likely to look ahead – to predict financial performance – than specific measures. Overall GFS satisfaction, for example, does not predict financial performance, whereas teller quality predicts financial performance for GFS's retail branches but does not apply outside of the branch banking system.

Sometimes measurement error is reduced by combining several specific measures into a composite measure. Composite measures like the branch-quality index are not generic measures but, rather, apply to particular businesses or functions like the specific measures from which they are formed. Composite measures, as a consequence, predict financial performance even better than specific measures but, like specific measures, usually cannot be rolled up from the bottom to the top of the organization.

Validate measures by testing the business model
The third step is validating measures by testing the business model statistically to identify non-financial measures actually predicting financial performance. Sears, it will be recalled from chapter 1, evaluated the impact of seventy measures of employee satisfaction and customer satisfaction on the financial performance of its retail stores before weighting these measures in compensation. The modeling exercise identified ten measures of employee and customer measures driving financial performance, and two-thirds of long-term compensation was then based on these measures. GFS, by contrast, chose PIP measures, the weights applied to PIP measures, and balanced scorecard measures before evaluating the impact of non-financial measures on the bottom-line performance of their branches. To be sure, GFS modified PIP and, to a lesser extent, balanced scorecard measures as experience accumulated, but GFS never undertook the kind of statistical analysis reported in the chapter.

Firms having a large number of similar business units like Sears and GFS can estimate the impact of non-financial measures on financial results and hence test business models statistically. Statistical tests will yield reliable results for firms with fewer than thirty or forty similar business units. And statistical tests are unlikely to be valid for diversified firms and for functionally organized firms whose units are highly dissimilar. Thus, many firms, perhaps the majority, will be unable to determine which non-financial measures predict financial performance, and hence will be unable to validate the business models implicit in their initial selection of measures.

Anticipate that measures will change

The last step in finding the right measures is anticipating that measures will change. One source of change is uncertainty: will unforeseeable changes or even changes that are foreseeable affect the non-financial measures predicting financial performance? Firms in stable industries that are not contemplating strategic changes (think of Envirosystems) are unlikely to encounter unforeseeable changes affecting the predictors of financial performance, whereas firms in industries perturbed by events like deregulation can anticipate that the predictors of financial performance will change dramatically. A second source of change is the running process described in chapter 2. The more attention focused on a performance measure, the greater the temptation to game the measure and drive variation and hence predictive power from it. The implication, of course, is that even the best measures must be reexamined from time to time.

Combining dissimilar measures

Choose between formulaic and subjective combination of measures

Firms normally rely on compensation formulas to combine financial and non-financial measures into an appraisal of overall performance and a bonus payout or salary adjustment. Pioneer Petroleum's scorecard-based incentive compensation plan, for example, combined five financial and eight non-financial measures by assigning explicit weights to each.[14] GFS, like Pioneer Petroleum, combined measures by assigning explicit weights to financial and non-financial measures under PIP. In both cases, measures were weighted explicitly before compensation decisions were made. GFS, unlike Pioneer Petroleum, later abandoned explicit weighting of measures by allowing measures to be combined subjectively under the balanced scorecard, that is, by weighting measures implicitly as compensation decisions were made. GFS's experience, then, suggests that firms have the choice of combining measures either formulaically where weights are explicit and assigned to measures ex ante or subjectively where weights are implicit and assigned to measures ex post.

Manage distortions caused by compensation formulas

Combining measures formulaically creates two kinds of distortions. One, which was observed at GFS, is outright gaming of measures: people achieve high levels of performance where targets can be met easily (for example, sales) while ignoring more difficult targets (for example, profitability). The most common corrective is setting minimum thresholds for all performance measures and then withholding bonuses or salary increments for people failing to meet any of these thresholds. GFS, in fact, took this approach under PIP, but the bonus formulas that resulted became so complicated that PIP had to be abandoned after three years. A second distortion is caused by inattention to measures whose percentage weightings in compensation formulas are small. Two of Pioneer Petroleum's five financial measures and five of its eight non-financial measures were weighted 3 percent or less – in all, seven of Pioneeer Petroleum's thirteen scorecard measure accounted for only 19 percent of compensation. It is hard to imagine that executives would pay much attention to these measures when margins, return on equity, and cost management accounted for 54 percent of their compensation. Whether or not these distortions can be fully managed is unclear. Gaming can be managed to some extent by replacing measures where targets are too easily met, and inattention to measures with small percentage weightings can be managed by consolidating measures weighted less than 10 percent. The challenge, of course, is maintaining balanced performance measurement while continually replacing and consolidating measures.

Manage distortions caused by subjectivity

Combining measures subjectively creates different distortions. One distortion is diminished expectancies: subjectivity in appraising and compensating performance will lead people to believe that rewards have become disconnected from measured performance. This disconnection will weaken people's motivation and, ultimately, cause their actual performance to decline. Majority agreement with the statement "When it comes to scorecard bonuses, I have no idea who gets what or why" suggests that performance-to-outcome expectancies declined as a result of GFS's implementation of the balanced scorecard. A second

distortion caused by subjectivity is reversion to unbalanced measurement – whether inadvertently or deliberately, the implicit weighting
of financial performance increases while the weightings attached to
non-financial measures decline. When subjectivity causes reversion to
unbalanced measurement, a firm incurs all of the costs of balanced performance measurement, including diminished expectancies and motivation, while realizing none of the benefits of balance. Two steps are
needed to manage the distortions caused by subjectivity. First, absent a
compensation formula, appraisals and compensation decisions must be
explained to people affected by them. These explanations need not be
entirely consistent. All that matters is that people understand the connection between their performance, the appraisal of their performance,
and their compensation. Second, absent a compensation formula, there
is only one way to detect whether reversion to unbalanced measurement has occurred: determine statistically whether non-financial measures have been factored into appraisals and bonuses, and then recalibrate appraisals and bonuses if necessary.

Anticipate that the performance measurement system will change
Distortions will occur whether measures are combined formulaically
or subjectively. While these distortions can be partially managed, they
cannot be managed completely because of the refractory nature of people. Any compensation formula will be gamed. It would be irrational
for people not to game formulas on which their livelihoods depend. Any
perception of subjectivity in appraising and compensating performance
will cause people to experience uncertainty and their expectancies and
motivation to perform will decline as a consequence. It would be irrational for people not to experience uncertainty when they cannot
perceive the connection between their performance, their appraisal,
and their compensation. The experience of GFS confirms that these
distortions cannot be managed completely. In six years, GFS moved
from purely financial performance measurement to a scorecard-like
system, PIP, where financial and non-financial measures were combined formulaically, to an implementation of the balanced scorecard
where measures were combined subjectively, and, recently, back to a
purely financial performance measurement system where only sales and
margins count. The question raised by this analysis and the experience
of GFS is whether any system aiming for balanced performance measurement can remain stable for long. Somewhat differently, is it not

reasonable to anticipate that all performance measurement systems will evolve and sometimes change dramatically, partly as a result of improved measurement techniques, but partly as a result of distortions occurring as people either learn to manipulate measures to their advantage or find that they cannot do so and hence lose their motivation to perform?

A brief summary

Balanced performance measurement is an attractive idea that can be difficult to implement. The notion of balance asserts that non-financial performance measures containing information about future financial performance should supplement financial measures in appraising and compensating performance. Balanced performance measurement, however, requires more: not only must non-financial measures predicting financial performance be found, but financial and non-financial measures, which are inherently dissimilar, must be combined into an overall appraisal of performance and a compensation decision. The case of GFS illustrates the challenges of meeting these requirements. GFS tried two versions of the balanced scorecard, one formulaic, the other subjective, and found neither satisfactory.

If not the balanced scorecard, how should performance be measured and compensated? The choices are unattractive because the problem of combining dissimilar measures into a single appraisal of performance transcends the balanced scorecard – recall from chapter 1 the tension between the proliferation of measures and the compression principle in measurement. The alternative that chapter 4 will introduce reduces the number of measures but increases the intensity of measurement by shifting the locus of measurement from firms and business units to customers and the most granular unit of all, the activities performed by the firm. This shift will initially seem awkward because performance measurement is often motivated by the need to appraise the performance of firms and, within firms, people. I shall argue, however, that appraising the performance of firms and their people requires answers to two prior questions: what are the activities in which the firm is engaged, and what are the economic consequences of these activities? Entrepreneurial firms like Envirosystems can answer these questions intuitively. What remains to be seen is whether large firms can address and answer these questions.

The bottom line

This chapter presented an account of the implementation of the balanced scorecard in the Western region of Global Financial Services. The general principles revealed by the analysis of GFS's efforts to implement balanced scorecards to appraise and compensate performance include the following:

- A balanced set of performance measures will include financial measures and non-financial measures adding information about economic performance not contained in financial measures. In other words, balanced measurement includes financial measures and non-financial measures that look ahead. This requirement holds whether balanced scorecards are used for strategic measurement or to appraise and compensate performance.
- When the balanced scorecards are to appraise and compensate performance, managers must, in addition to finding the right measures, combine dissimilar measures into overall appraisal of performance. This can be difficult to do. Combining measures by formula encourages people to game the formula by delivering everything but bottom-line performance. Combining measures subjectively limits gaming, but it creates uncertainty, consumes a great deal of time, and ultimately undermines motivation.
- Two requirements of balanced performance measurement, then, are finding the right measures and combining these measures into an overall appraisal and then compensating performance. Finding the right measures requires finding non-financial measures actually – not just potentially – driving financial results and likely to drive financial results going forward. Many firms, like GFS, will find this difficult to do. Combining measures creates distortions – gaming of compensation formulas, or uncertainty arising from subjectivity – that must be managed. Again many firms, like GFS, will find this difficult to do.
- The requirements of balanced performance measurement suggest that balanced scorecards should be used to monitor progress toward strategic objectives but not to appraise and compensate performance.

Postscript: From balanced performance measurement to a sales-focused strategy

In early 1999, new management took control of GFS's US retail operations and immediately changed the strategy of the business. The five "imperatives" enunciated in 1995 were replaced by a sales-focused strategy aimed at producing dramatic improvement in earnings. Toward this end, all costs were scrutinized and the expense base of GFS's retail operations was cut by more than 20 percent. Revenue growth was sought through increased fees and aggressive promotion of fee-based products (such as insurance and investments) with somewhat less emphasis on traditional asset (loan) and liability (demand deposit) products. Branch employees other than tellers were required to obtain licenses to sell insurance and investments, and the compensation of all employees was based on meeting sales or sales-related targets, the latter including referrals of customers to relationship managers licensed to sell investment products. Needless to say, customer satisfaction figured less prominently under the new strategy. Customer satisfaction surveys continued with greatly reduced samples through the end of 1999 and were then abandoned altogether. The balanced scorecard was abandoned as well.

The sales-focused strategy had an immediate impact on the bottom-line income of GFS's US retail business. Return on assets before restructuring charges skyrocketed from 1.1 to 4.1 percent from 1998 to 1999. Much of this increase in ROA was due to the cost reductions implemented by the new management. Cost reductions together with a reduction in the provision for credit losses accounted for 73 percent of the 1998–99 increase in pretax income of US retail operations.

The long-run sustainability of these results will depend on the impact of the new strategy on GFS's retail customers. Decomposing bottom-line earnings into revenue and expenditure components and then decomposing the revenue component into fee and balance revenues can help us understand how this impact will operate. Balance revenues, in turn, can be further decomposed into the product of actual balances and spreads, the latter the difference between GFS's cost of funds, which is the interest rate GFS's treasury charges its operating units,[15] and the interest earned on funds. The full decomposition of earnings is sketched in figure 3.8. Figure 3.8 also shows how customer retention, the difference between rates of customer acquisition and attrition, is likely to affect fee and balance revenues separately. The solid arrow running from customer retention to balance revenues indicates that a close relationship between the two is expected, in other words, that balance revenues will accrue to the extent that customers and their balances are retained. By contrast, the dotted line from customer retention to fee-based revenues indicates that a weaker relationship between retention

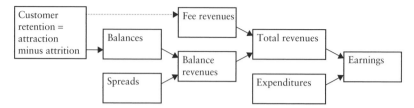

Figure 3.8 Decomposition of earnings

and revenues is expected since sales of fee-based products like insurance may be one-time transactions not depending on sustained customer relationships.[16]

Data describing a sample of GFS branches in the Eastern and Western regions allow limited assessment of the impact of the new strategy on customer retention and hence the likely impact on fee and balance revenues. Some thirty GFS branches, eighteen in the Eastern and twelve in the Western region, are represented in this sample. The thirty are intended to be representative of the two regions but not of GFS's entire US retail operations. Monthly series on customer attraction and attrition by segment and product as well as balances, spreads, and revenues by product are available for each branch from July through December 1999. The overall picture painted by these data is uneven. In the second half of 1999, customer attrition exceeded attraction in both the consumer and small business segments. To illustrate: the thirty branches acquired 37,000 consumer households[17] but lost 52,000 consumer households from July to December 1999. During the same period these branches acquired 2300 but lost 3700 small business customers, which are generally more profitable than consumer households. The same pattern of attrition exceeding acquisition held for most individual products and especially for mutual funds accounts held by consumers. The thirty branches added 1700 consumer mutual fund accounts from July to December 1999 but lost 5800 of them. There are exceptions to the overall pattern: for example, the thirty branches gained more than 5000 consumer money market checking accounts while losing fewer than 2000 in this period.[18] All of these results hold when customer acquisition and attrition data are examined separately for GFS's Eastern and Western regions.

Despite the overall loss of retail and small business customers in the thirty sample branches, revenues from fees and balances, the latter with spreads held constant, grew marginally from July through December 1999. The relevant data are displayed in figure 3.9. As can be seen,

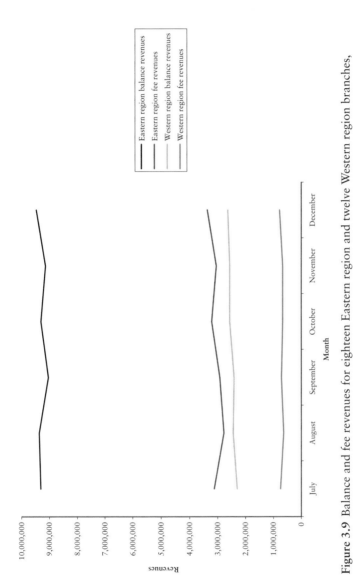

Figure 3.9 Balance and fee revenues for eighteen Eastern region and twelve Western region branches, July–December 1999. Balance revenues are computed using July 1999 spreads; all revenue are in US$.

there are slight differences between the Eastern and Western regions. In the Eastern region, balance revenues as well as fee revenues were essentially flat until December 1999, when both increased by 4–5 percent. In the Western region, balance revenues grew steadily throughout the six-month period while fee revenues remained essentially flat. In neither region do we observe the pattern anticipated as a consequence of net customer attrition – flat to declining balance revenues coupled with growing fee revenues.

There is a simple lesson and a subtler lesson. The simple lesson is that cutting costs and implementing a sales-focused strategy in place of the balanced scorecard improved bottom-line income dramatically. Even customer attrition in excess of acquisition did not cause short-run revenues to decline, although it remains unclear how economic and competitive conditions may have influenced this result. The subtler lesson, which is important for the activity-based profitability analysis (ABPA), is that it is difficult to trace the consequences for the bottom line of any action taken by a firm absent customer-by-customer profitability data. The data just reviewed described GFS's branches, not GFS's customers. They describe the total number of customers (and customer accounts) acquired and lost as well as balance and fee revenues for thirty branches over a six-month period. They are typical of the performance data available to most middle and senior managers in large firms. And they are ambiguous because they do not tell us whether the sales-focused strategy improved GFS's performance. What we learn from them is that GFS lost customers and, in the short run, made money.

If customer-by-customer profitability data were available, it would be much easier to appraise the impact of the sales-focused strategy on GFS's performance. What data are available show that GFS suffered net customer attrition following implementation of the new strategy even though GFS did not suffer loss of revenues. Whether the sales-focused strategy caused GFS to lose (or gain) its most profitable, marginally profitable, potentially profitable, or unprofitable customers is not known.

4 | *From cost drivers to revenue drivers*

T HE task at the heart of the performance measurement problem is finding the precursors of future cash flows – or, equivalently, the long-term viability and efficiency of the firm. Let us begin this chapter with a question: When are the drivers of costs also the drivers of revenues? All managers from time to time face a related question: where can we cut costs without impairing revenues, and where can we ill afford to cut costs because revenues will be impaired? This question is especially crucial in the context of global management, since success in the global marketplace often requires driving unit costs downward relentlessly. If there were simple ways to cut costs without impairing revenues, much of the performance-measurement problem would disappear, and many of the tough choices facing managers would be easier. But there are no simple solutions. Separating costs that should be managed aggressively from costs that must be tolerated because they are incurred by critical revenue drivers can be very difficult.

This chapter develops a new approach to performance measurement, activity-based profitability analysis (ABPA). ABPA is founded on a simple premise: if you understand the activities in which the firm engages, their costs, and the revenues that result from them, then you have a powerful tool for measuring and improving the performance of the firm.

ABPA is based on the elemental conception of the firm that defines the performance of a firm as what the firm does, its activities, and the measure of performance as the revenues generated by these activities less the cost of performing them. ABPA is derived from an established performance measurement technique, activity-based costing (ABC). It is also based on a success story, the success many firms have had in managing costs using ABC. ABPA maps almost everything the firm does onto bottom-line results, avoiding many of the problems associated with measures of non-financial performance. ABPA exhibits all the complexity of activity-based costing and then some, and it is not yet proven. But it is still an approach worth exploring.

From activity-based costing to activity-based profitability analysis

Activity-based profitability analysis is grounded in activity-based costing, which is a granular form of costing: it identifies the actual costs of labor, materials, equipment, and premises needed to deliver a product, serve the customer, and sustain the business. ABC practitioners believe that making costs known creates opportunities for savings even though ABC methodology alone does not identify savings targets. Two advantages are claimed for ABC compared to conventional costing methods. First, ABC makes all costs explicit, reducing distortions caused by arbitrary allocations of overhead to products and customers. Second, ABC traces costs back to the economic events that cause them, making it possible to judge the reasonableness of costs in light of these events.

The following example illustrates the difference between ABC and conventional costing methods. Conventionally, the cost of assembling a circuit board is calculated as the direct cost of labor and materials costs plus indirect costs, the latter a percentage of direct costs – in highly automated processes, these percentages can be 500 percent or more. There is no way of knowing whether the cost of assembling a circuit board so calculated is accurate and, if it is accurate, whether savings can be realized. Under ABC, by contrast, all of the costs involved in assembling a circuit board and the economic events driving these costs are recognized explicitly. Hence there are few if any indirect costs that cannot be controlled. For example, one of the principal costs of assembling circuit boards is chip insertion. The number of chip insertions is determined by the design of the board. The cost of each chip insertion is a function of the labor, premises, and equipment costs of inserting a single chip. In the argot of ABC, circuit board assembly is the cost object, the number of chip insertions is the cost driver, the cost of inserting a single chip is the activity cost, and the activity (that is, the economic event incurring costs) is chip insertion. While all of this language sounds complex, tracing board assembly costs back to the economic events like chip insertions allows circuit board designers to ask whether savings can be realized by substituting integrated chips for discrete components. Though integrated chips are more expensive than equivalent discrete components, decreasing the frequency of chip insertions usually offsets the higher cost of integrated chips.

Activity-based costing is less useful when costing decisions are made without objective information about their consequences. Imagine, if you can, removing costs from circuit board assembly not knowing how the functionality and reliability of assembled boards will be affected. The chances are high that the circuit boards will fail and you will quickly be out of business. It is for this reason that most applications of ABC are in manufacturing or in service industries such as parcel delivery where product specifications constrain costing decisions.

ABPA extends ABC by seeking to understand the revenue consequences of activities alongside costs. ABPA focuses initially on the customer as the point where costs and revenues intersect. ABPA asks the apparently naïve question: what do we do for the customer that generates revenues in excess of costs? Panel (a) of figure 4.1 shows the path from activities to revenues. The path originates with activities. Activities add value for the customer, and value added in turn drives customer revenues. In two respects this diagram is more subtle than the apparently naïve question that motivated it. First, as shown, the relationship between activities and revenues is mediated by value added for the customer. This occurs because many activities – those performed without charge, those bundled and performed on demand for a flat fee or no fee – do not yield revenues directly. Second, because value added for the customer cannot be observed, the revenues attributable to each activity performed for the customer must be estimated in a causal model. Such a model is sketched in panel (b) of figure 4.1. The model, of course, is only a set of hypotheses. The contribution of activities to revenues must be estimated by analyzing the relevant data.

The ABC view of the relationship of costs to revenues is different. As shown in italics in figure 4.1, ABC establishes activity costs and then *customer* profitability by comparing the costs of performing activities for each customer with the revenues supplied by the customer. The approach suggested here establishes also activity costs using ABC, but it then establishes activity revenues by estimating the contribution of activities to customer revenues, and the profitability of each activity by comparing activity revenues with activity costs.

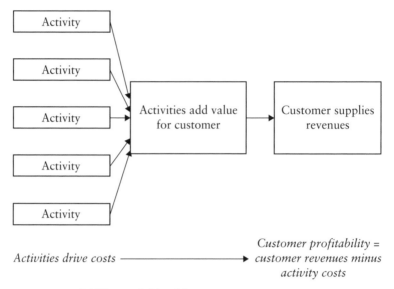

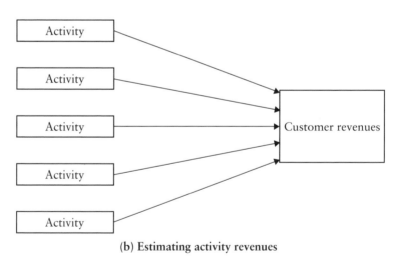

(a) **How activities drive customer revenues**
(**ABC view in italics**)

(b) **Estimating activity revenues**

Figure 4.1 The impact of activities on customer revenues

At this point, let us back up to examine in some detail the circumstances where costing decisions can be made without explicit knowledge of their revenue consequences and where it is critical to understand the revenue consequences of costing decisions.

Products whose value is captured in specifications

Some simple examples illustrate where it is important to separate cost drivers from revenue drivers and where it is not. Consider first a product whose value to the customer depends entirely on physical specifications such as capacity, reliability, and speed – in other words, a product whose value depends on its functionality or performance for the customer, not its economic performance. Such a product might be a desktop computer or, better, the memory chips (DRAMs) inside the computer. For commodity products like DRAMs, all that counts for the customer is price and speed: the latter is the measure of functionality. Panel (a) of figure 4.2 illustrates the separation of cost drivers from revenue drivers for products like DRAMs. There are three elements in this figure: the activities involved in manufacturing the product (five are shown, but manufacturing usually involves more), the product itself, and the resulting specifications (three are shown, probably too many). Note that the product is split by a dashed vertical line. This line signifies that the activities involved in manufacturing a product can be separated from product specifications and measured independently. Note too that manufacturing activities incur costs – activities are cost drivers – while the specifications add value for the customer – specifications are revenue drivers.

The challenge facing makers of DRAMs and similar products is to find ways to eliminate activities and hence costs from manufacturing while maintaining or augmenting the physical specifications of the product and hence value for the customer. Manufacturers of DRAMs (and desktop PCs) failing to drive costs rapidly downward while improving the functionality of their products have been competed out of business. The lesson here, though, isn't that costs must be reduced regardless. Quite the opposite. It's that it is easiest to reduce costs when revenues are driven by product specifications – the performance of the product for the customer – which can be maintained or improved even as unnecessary activities are eliminated.

Products not made to specifications

Now compare DRAMs to a product whose value to the customer cannot be reduced to a set of specifications distinct from the activities that comprise it, such as an airline journey.[1] An airline journey

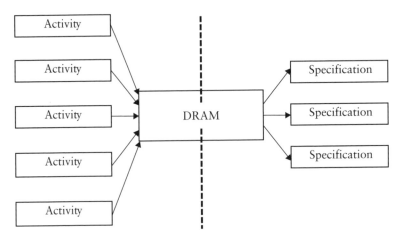

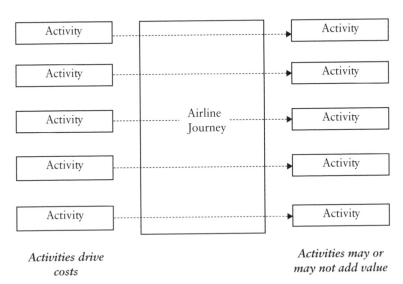

Figure 4.2 Separating cost drivers from revenue drivers: the need for product specifications

involves a bundle of activities that touch the customer – ticketing, boarding, on-board service (of which there are several components), baggage handling, and facilities upon arrival (a shower, a limousine), and frequent-flyer incentives. There are two interesting features of the bundle of activities comprising an airline journey. First, any of these activities may add value for the customer, but many do not. Second, the activities adding value may vary from customer to customer or, for that matter, from flight to flight. Long-haul passengers may find value in the availability of a business-class boarding lounge, the attentiveness of cabin staff, and the quality of arrival facilities; short-haul passengers, by contrast, may find value in the quality of peanuts served in flight and little else. Thus, revenue drivers cannot easily be separated from cost drivers for products that are not reducible to one or two specifications like airline journeys. This occurs because, as shown in panel (b) of figure 4.2, the same bundle of activities that drives costs may also drive revenues, but the impact of activities on revenues is not known. Lacking product specifications clearly separable from the activities required to produce and deliver a product, it is difficult to maintain or improve the product while eliminating activities from it. Costs will creep upward until expenses must be cut across unselectively. The recent history of British Airways is illustrative. Since BA privatized in the late 1980s, its strategy has been to provide high levels of customer service. Toward this end, BA has tracked and improved more than 300 elements of customer service ranging from the length of queues at airport counters to satisfaction with the handling of complaints. BA has performed well for its customers and is regularly voted one of Europe's best companies. But BA has also had difficulty maintaining a competitive cost structure, and there have been periodic cost reductions.

Clearly, firms delivering complex services like BA must find a different solution to the problem of separating cost drivers from revenue drivers so that they can improve productivity by constraining the former while augmenting the latter. This can only be accomplished by changing fundamentally the way in which the problem of separating cost from revenue drivers is construed. Until now, the problem has been construed as one of removing costs from products and services without removing value from them. The solution to this problem has been to treat product specifications as proxies for value and then to remove costs while preserving specifications. This approach is effective so long as product specifications exist apart from the activities needed to produce the product. But this approach is not effective where the product is a service manufactured as it is delivered. In services, it is often nearly impossible to distinguish the activities involved in producing the product from the product itself. Nor, by extension, is this approach effective for businesses continuously delivering products to customers – in other words, businesses driven by ongoing customer relationships – because it is difficult to understand which products, and hence which product specifications, add value for the customer and which do not.

A comparison of the upper panels of figures 4.1 and 4.2 is instructive. Both figures begin with activities – in other words, activities are inputs in both cases. In figure 4.1, activities influence the customer to make choices that have revenue (as well as cost) consequences. In figure 4.2, however, activities shape products whose specifications, if specifications exist, are assumed but not demonstrated to add value for the customer. Thus, while customer revenues are the outputs in figure 4.1, product specifications are the outputs in figure 4.2. A further difference between figures 4.1 and 4.2 is in the way that connections between inputs and outputs are established. In figure 4.1, connections between input activities and customer revenue outputs cannot be established by design since it is difficult to anticipate how customers will value different activities. In figure 4.2, connections between input activities and output specifications are fixed in the design of the manufacturing or service process. These connections, instead, must be established from experience, usually from statistical inferences drawn from the behavior of customers.

The most important difference between figures 4.1 and 4.2, however, is in the kinds of insights activity-based costing (ABC) can generate. In figure 4.1, ABC identifies the cost of activities directly and their contribution to revenues indirectly *provided the costs incurred and the revenues generated by each customer are known*. In figure 4.2, ABC identifies the cost of activities but not the contribution of activities to revenues since revenues are not measured. What is unique about figure 4.1, then, is the matching of activities performed for each customer and the activity costs these activities incur with the revenues generated by each customer.

Time-sensitive products

It can also be difficult to manage costs when a product or service has precise specifications but their long-run impact on value for the customer, and hence on revenues, may differ from their short-run impact. Think of any distribution system or supply chain whose output is described by such specifications as the percentage of on-time deliveries and frequency of out-of-stock conditions. Costs are the direct costs of transporting and warehousing goods, the cost of carrying inventories, and costs incurred due to price deterioration or "rot" while goods are in the distribution system. (More than one computer maker tells its people, "We make bananas.")

Supply chain managers seek to minimize total distribution costs while having goods available at all times: the easy but expensive way to insure that goods are in stock is to maintain large inventories. This is a matter of optimizing the design of the system, which is no mean feat but can be done analytically.[2] Supply chain managers also seek to understand how the customer values the performance of the distribution system. Most managers, for example, believe that customers prefer to find goods in stock rather than out of stock. But when a large computer manufacturer, whom I will call Abacus Computers, tested this proposition, they found little support for it.

Abacus borrowed the sales floor of a large retailer and simulated four conditions: both Abacus and competitors' products in stock, Abacus in stock but competitors out of stock, Abacus out of stock but competitors in stock, and both Abacus and competitors out of stock. The critical comparison was between the first and third conditions where competitors' products were in stock. Abacus customers turned out to be extremely loyal even when Abacus products were out of stock. Almost uniformly, customers who intended to buy the Abacus product but learned it was out of stock left the store without making a purchase.

The lesson learned was not the lesson anticipated. Abacus had hoped to learn how retail customers value the performance of its distribution system. What Abacus actually learned was that most of its customers are very loyal and willing to forgive poor performance of the distribution system – once. Whether customers would forgive persistent poor performance in distribution is a different matter. Abacus, like any sensible business, is reluctant to find out what would happen if its products were perennially out of stock.

The upshot is that cost drivers can be separated from revenue drivers when two conditions obtain: (1) products or services are made to physical specifications, and (2) these specifications capture performance for the customer and hence drive revenues. When both of these conditions prevail, costs can be reduced so long as specifications are maintained or improved (e.g.DRAMs). But only rarely are both of these conditions present. For many products and services, there are no specifications (an extreme case is psychotherapy). For others, the activities that drive costs are in effect specifications that may or may not add value for the customer and hence drive revenues – in other words, activities and specifications cannot be distinguished (e.g. airline journeys). Even where specifications exist and are separable from activities, such specifications may have little impact on short-run value for the customer even though their long-run impact on value may be substantial (e.g. Abacus' supply-chain metrics). To put it differently: the more commodity-like the product and the less the significance of ongoing customer relationships, the easier it is to separate cost drivers from revenue drivers. The reverse is also true: the less commodity-like the product and the greater the significance of customer relationships, the more difficult it is to separate the two.

The nuts and bolts of activity-based profitability analysis

The firm's functioning and its economic results intersect in the relationship of the firm to the customer. The firm performs activities to meet customer requirements, these activities incur costs, and the customer supplies revenues. It follows that connections between activities, costs, and revenues are best understood at the level of customers rather than business units or the firm as a whole. In the language of the social sciences, the customer is the unit of analysis; in the language of business, the customer is the profit center.

Once the customer is the unit of analysis or the profit center, it is fairly easy to connect activities and activity costs, on the one hand, with revenues and profitability, on the other. Figure 4.3 illustrates how this is done in financial services where products consist of transactions of various types. The customer is at the center of figure 4.3. Working leftward from the customer, customers initiate transactions that in turn trigger support transactions.[3] Both customer-initiated and customer-support transactions involve direct and indirect activities.[4] Activities incur three kinds of costs, short-term variable costs, long-term variable costs, and capacity costs.[5] Working rightward from the customer, customer net revenue flows from customers,[6] and customer profitability is customer net revenues less transaction costs. Note also in figure 4.3 that product costs are almost incidental. In financial services, products

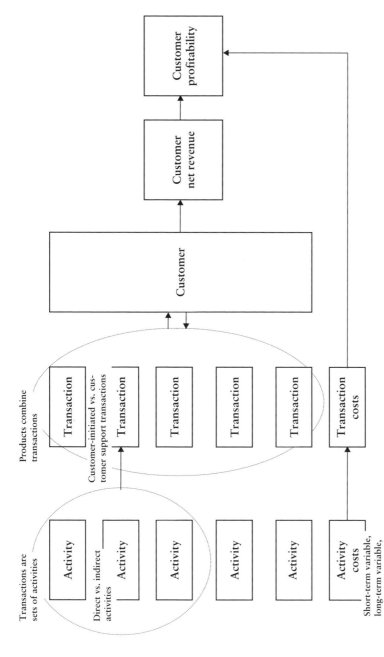

Figure 4.3 ABPA connects customer transactions, activity costs, and customer profitability

are sets of transactions, some more intricate than others, and product costs, therefore, are simply the sum of the costs of transactions required to deliver the product.

The system described in figure 4.3 is unusual in two respects. It shows, first, that there is no *necessary* connection between transactions and transaction costs, on the one hand, and revenues, on the other. The bulk of revenues accrue when transactions add value for customers, and customers, as a consequence, maintain balances that yield revenues far greater than transaction fees. Second, the system generates data on transaction frequencies, transaction costs, revenues, and profitability *for each customer* in real time. In other words, the system doesn't merely reveal transaction costs and customer profitability, which ABC does conventionally. It also connects profits with transactions *customer by customer*. These data make it possible to describe not only the customer's relationship with the organization – the transactions and products utilized by the customer – but also the long-term profitability of this relationship since the system operates in real time. Moreover, by breaking down the customer relationship transaction by transaction, these data allow the long-term profitability of each type of transaction to be estimated as well.

ABPA opens some promising opportunities. Figure 4.3 suggests several. One is the opportunity to identify inexpensive transactions and products, package them, and sell them at several times cost. Another is the opportunity to identify unprofitable customers and either reprice them or encourage them to take their business elsewhere. But the opportunity to discover which transactions and products – that is, which customer relationships – are profitable in the long run may be more important than identifying inexpensive products and customers who are currently profitable.

Discovering the transactions and products contributing to profitable customer relationships is critical for several reasons. There is an economic advantage: transactions and products contributing to profitable relationships can be promoted, while transactions and products detracting from profitability can be discouraged or rationalized. There is also a competitive advantage: while it is easy for competitors to imitate the products you produce inexpensively and to undercut your margins by competing on price, it is very difficult for competitors to understand which products to sell to which customers profitably – constructing a system that allows you to understand this is no small feat, and the profitability estimates the system generates are proprietary.

Figure 4.4, which is a simplification of figure 4.3, shows how transactions and products contributing to profitable customer relationships can be identified and then refined so as to become even more profitable. Figure 4.4 suggests two steps. The first step is to estimate current customer profitability – *current* customer net revenue less the cost of *current* transactions and products – as a function of *prior* transactions and product utilization. It is important to lag transactions and product utilization because it takes time for their full revenue consequences to develop. It does not matter how these revenue consequences develop; hence the simplicity of figure 4.4. What does matter is whether the revenue consequences of transactions and products are positive, zero, or worse. The second step is to reconfigure transactions and products to maximize the profitability of customer relationships. This can be accomplished by encouraging the use of specific transactions and products and discouraging or repricing others. This is the essence of ABPA, which relies on activity-based costing to estimate the profitability of each customer and then separates products and services contributing to customer profitability from those incurring costs.

An example illustrating the opportunities presented by ABPA may be helpful. The most frequent transactions in the retail business of GFS (the global financial services firm we met in the last chapter) in a Latin American country are depositing checks and clearing checks. Next most frequent are balance inquiries – there are 500,000 balance inquiries a month, or nearly five inquiries per account, an artifact of the region's history of hyperinflation. The unit cost of balance inquiries as estimated by ABC varies, from a few cents if directed to a centralized automated voice-response unit to several dollars if directed to branch relationship officers. Since customers direct about half of their balance inquiries to the automated unit and half to relationship officers, the cost of balance inquiries is in vicinity of $1 million a month. The question is whether this level of expenditure is excessive – in the argot of ABC, whether balance inquiries are overfunded – and, in particular, whether balance inquiries should be diverted to the automated unit.

The sales force believes that balance inquiries are also sales opportunities for relationship officers: according to the sales force, the revenues ultimately flowing from balance inquiries far exceed the costs they incur. Others are skeptical, noting that customers with the lowest

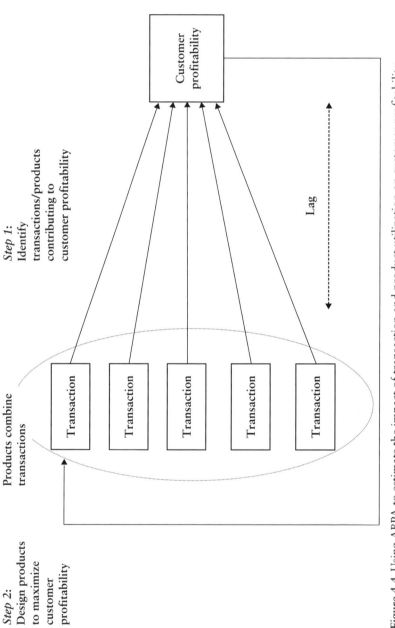

Figure 4.4 Using ABPA to estimate the impact of transaction and product utilization on customer profitability

balances, and hence the lowest revenues, are most likely to inquire about their balances. The virtue of the ABPA framework illustrated in figure 4.4 is that it is capable of discriminating between customers for whom balance inquiries yield revenues in excess of costs and those for whom such costs exceed revenues. In other words, ABPA can ascertain not only whether balance inquiries are profitable or unprofitable overall but also whether balance inquiries are profitable for some customer segments and not for others. The exact form of the relationship between balance inquiries and subsequent revenues net of costs need not be specified here. What is important, and what makes the problem manageable, is that lags between balance inquiries and their effects on revenues should be fairly short, consistent with the sales force's argument that balance inquiries are also sales opportunities.

From ABC to ABPA: a case in point

The experience of Global Financial Services illustrates what happens when ABC is used to analyze costs, which it does fairly objectively, but costing decisions are then made subjectively because their consequences for revenues are not understood. GFS's Country A retail business is fairly large, about 100,000 customers and revenues of about $200 million. Country A was plagued by hyperinflation through the early 1990s but then reformed its currency and stabilized wages and prices. GFS initially adapted to the new environment by growing its retail customer base in Country A dramatically. But GFS took on more customers than its staff and systems could serve effectively. Customer satisfaction and profits plummeted, and management decided in mid-1992 to prune unprofitable customers and to initiate a quality program. Both were major projects. Pruning unprofitable customers required a measure of customer profitability, a measure that did not exist. Bolstering customer satisfaction required a quality organization capable of responding quickly and forcefully to customer complaints. This organization also did not exist.

Measuring customer profitability

To measure customer profitability, a batch system capturing revenues and a portion of variable costs for each customer was put in place by mid-1993.[7] The revenue calculation, called customer net revenue or

CNR, was routine – balances (both asset and liability) times interest-rate spreads, plus fees charged the customer. The calculation of variable costs was more difficult because it required a system capable of recording many different kinds of customer transactions, for example opening an account, making a deposit, purchasing a mutual fund, or making a complaint. Unit costs were estimated for each type of transaction using a crude form of ABC; variable costs were computed for each customer as the frequency of each type of transaction times its unit cost; and variable costs were compared to CNR for each customer monthly. The resulting figure was an estimate of customer profitability. Customers were then classified into three categories: (1) revenues greater than fixed plus variable costs, (2) revenues greater than variable costs but less than fixed plus variable costs, and (3) revenues less than variable costs. Customers falling into the third category were then repriced in the expectation that they would either become profitable or take their business elsewhere. Management was surprised to find that revenues were below variable costs for many of their largest customers. They should not have been – ABC often reveals that the largest customers are the least profitable because they command low margins and incur high service costs.[8]

Managing customer complaints

Customer satisfaction was managed by creating a quality organization that implemented a rigorous problem-resolution process. A toll-free phone number was established to provide customers direct access to the quality organization. The quality organization contacted customers who were dissatisfied with the way their complaints had been handled. All customer complaints were analyzed and zero-defect teams were dispatched in most instances to find and correct the root cause of the problem. These steps immediately and dramatically improved customer satisfaction.[9] Problem incidence and internal investigations resulting from customer complaints improved just as dramatically.[10]

The magnitude of these improvements is evident in internal data on problem incidence and problem resolution across GFS's seven Latin American markets. As shown in table 4.1, in December 1994 the percentage of customers reporting problems in Country A was 8 percent – less than half that of other Latin American markets, where the figures ranged from 18 to 21 percent. Problem-resolution satisfaction was

Table 4.1 *Country A quality measures (by percentage)*

	June 1992	December 1992	December 1993	December 1994
Overall GFS satisfaction (top 2 boxes, 5-point scale)	71	85	95	
Overall GFS satisfaction – new accounts	72	89	92	
Recommend GFS	77	81	97	
Problem incidence (percentage of accounts)	42	27	9	8
Problem resolution satisfaction (top 2 boxes)	32	50	65	95
Inquiries and investigations per 1000 accounts		7.8	2.7	1.6

95 percent in Country A (versus 43 to 65 percent elsewhere). The number of investigations opened per 1000 accounts was 1.6 per month in Country A (versus 3.9 to 17.3 per thousand in other markets). Perhaps as cause and perhaps as consequence of the small number of investigations, the cost per investigation in Country A was substantially higher than in other Latin American markets: $57 per investigation in Country A compared to $3 to $29 per investigation elsewhere. More significantly, perhaps, by the end of 1994 voluntary customer attrition was 0.1 percent per month in Country A versus 0.6 to 5.0 percent in GFS's other Latin American markets.

Assessing costs of the problem-resolution process

In early 1995 GFS turned its attention from quality to costs as the business environment became more competitive. A consultant was engaged to do activity-based costing for the entire business in the expectation that ABC would identify opportunities for savings. Guided by the consultant, an ABC team initially identified several hundred activities and their costs, and then classified activities into five categories: correctly funded, underfunded, overfunded (necessary but too expensive), overperformed (necessary but performed excessively), and not necessary. The team also recommended cost reductions for activities falling into the overfunded and overperformed categories – unnecessary activities were slated for 100 percent expenditure reductions – with an overall cost savings target of 7–8 percent in mind. Several of the ABC team's recommendations focused on the quality process and, in particular, expenditures incurred by the activities of the quality organization. For example, zero-defect team leadership – middle-management oversight of zero-defect teams – was classified as an unnecessary activity and targeted for elimination. Quality research management – design and analysis of customer surveys – was classified as overperformed and targeted for a 50 percent cost reduction. Problem resolution was also classified as overperformed and targeted for a 20 percent reduction.

Senior management hired a second consultant to resolve discrepancies between the ABC team's recommendations and the internal data on problem resolution just reviewed. This consultant convened the ABC team, divided the team into two focus groups, one more senior than the other, and asked both groups to reconstruct the process that led them to classify several activities as unnecessary or overperformed. Not surprisingly, the two groups perceived the process somewhat differently. The differences were especially sharp with respect to the classification of zero-defect team leadership as unnecessary. The more senior group believed that middle management oversight of the quality process was no longer needed because quality was deeply embedded in the organization:

We told [GFS] how important quality is two years ago. Today [GFS] understands quality. Leadership not important. The process is mature. Intermediate level of leadership is not necessary. We don't need coordination of quality at intermediate level – let subgroups work alone on quality.

The junior group, by contrast, was not confident that the quality process could function without middle management oversight:

We are not at all comfortable with this decision. We're not sure that [zero-defect team leadership] can be cut 100 percent. We don't have all the data needed to make this judgment.

The two groups were in much closer agreement as to why the problem-resolution activity was classified as overperformed. According to the more senior group: "There are fewer problems. As a consequence, problem resolution cost should decrease. We used data on the number of problems," while the junior group commented: "Our view is about the same. Reduced problem incidence accounts for cost reduction."

Note the difference in the way the two activities were evaluated. Zero-defect team leadership activity was evaluated subjectively – the more senior group, which prevailed, believed that zero-defect team leadership was redundant whereas the junior group was uncertain. The problem-resolution activity, by contrast, appears to have been evaluated objectively: the number of problems had been correlated with problem-resolution expenditures, and the latter had been judged excessive by both groups.

In fact, both of these judgments were based on incomplete data because the focus had been exclusively on costs. When shown the data in table 4.1, which compares problem incidence and problem resolution in Country A and other Latin American markets, the ABC team quickly understood that it had focused narrowly on the frequency and cost of investigations rather than comparing the costs of investigations with their benefits – high levels of customer satisfaction and low rates of customer attrition. The judgment of the ABC team with respect to zero-defect teams was unanimous: "We will have to rethink the conclusion that zero-defect team leadership is not necessary." Once they understood the complexity of this issue, as illustrated in figure 4.5, the team decided to reserve judgment on whether the problem-resolution activity was overperformed.

Linking activities to revenues with ABPA

Figure 4.5 combines the ABC perspective on the problem resolution activity with the broader perspective of activity-based profitability analysis or ABPA, which traces the revenue and hence the profitability consequences of problem resolution alongside its costs. The ABC perspective is shown on the left side of figure 4.5. The path from cost drivers to activities to costs is utterly straightforward: the frequency of the cost driver – inquiries and complaints – drives the frequency of problem-resolution activities, which in turn drive problem-resolution costs. The implication of the ABC perspective is equally straightforward: problem resolution costs should vary with the frequency of inquiries and complaints.

The ABPA perspective, on the right side of figure 4.5, shows that the path from cost drivers to activities to revenues is anything but straightforward. Inquiries and complaints lead to problem-resolution activities, to be sure, but there are then three distinct paths through

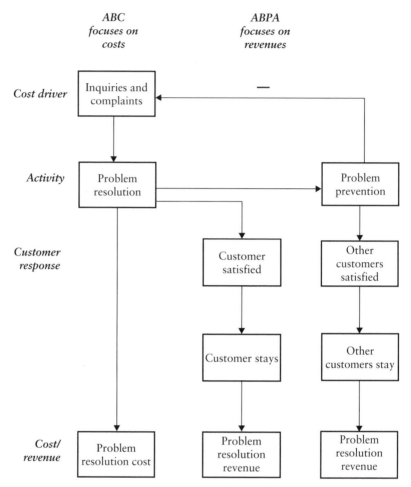

Figure 4.5 The cost and revenue consequences of problem resolution activity

which problem-resolution activities influence revenues. The first path is through the customer originating the inquiry or complaint: the customer is either satisfied or dissatisfied with the way the complaint is handled, and either remains or does not remain a customer. The second path is through other customers: problem prevention either occurs or does not occur as a result of the problem-resolution activity; the satisfaction of customers not voicing complaints either improves or does not improve as a result of problem prevention; and the likelihood that other customers will remain customers either increases or does not increase. The third path is through a feedback loop influencing the frequency of inquiries and complaints and hence revenues through the other two paths: problem prevention either occurs or does not occur as a result of problem-resolution activity, and problem prevention in turn either does or does not influence the frequency of inquiries and complaints.

The only firm conclusion to be drawn from figure 4.5 is that the costs of activities like problem resolution can be traced much more easily than their impact on revenues. This is the case for three reasons: (1) because costs are incurred as the activities are performed, whereas revenues accrue later; (2) because revenues depend on actions taken by customers whose actions can be unpredictable; and, in this instance, (3) because the feedback loop from problem prevention to inquiries and complaints adds a further complication. This said, it appears that problem-resolution activity within a reasonable range contributes positively to revenues.

While the full contribution of problem-resolution activity to revenues cannot be determined from the information at hand, one part of this contribution can be crudely estimated from table 4.2. Excluding Country E, which is an outlier because its economy was in turmoil, the correlation of the dollar cost per investigation with the monthly attrition rate of retail customers is 0.57.[11] A one dollar increase in the cost per investigation is estimated to decrease monthly customer attrition by 0.015 percentage points. Assuming that this result holds for Country A and that Country A decides to reduce the cost per investigation by $10, from $57 to $47 per investigation, the cost of investigations per 1000 accounts will then move from $89 to $73 monthly, but the monthly customer attrition rate is forecast to increase by 0.15 percent or 1.5 accounts per thousand. These results suggest that the savings in problem resolution expenditures recommended by the ABC team may be a false economy. Average monthly revenue per retail account is about $100. Reducing problem resolution costs by $16 per thousand accounts per month would increase attrition costs by approximately $150 per month. And this figure does not take into account the cost of replacing lost accounts or the likelihood of an increase in the frequency of inquiries and complaints.

The lesson of this case is that ABC can go awry when it focuses on activity drivers and activity costs and ignores the revenue consequences

Table 4.2 Problem incidence and problem resolution in Latin American markets

	Country A	Country B	Country C	Country D	Country E	Country F	Country G
Problem incidence (%)	8	18	21	20	18	19	
Problem resolution satisfaction (%)	95	65	43	47	60	53	
Inquiries and investigations per 1000 accounts	1.6	13.3	14.7	3.9	10.8	13.0	17.3
Cost per investigation ($)	57	6	4	14	11	29	3
Cost per 1000 accounts ($)	89	76	57	55	120	383	55
Monthly attrition rate (%)	0.1	1.6	0.9	0.6	5.0	1.5	1.0

of activities. In manufacturing and in service environments where processes can be blueprinted, specifications serve as surrogates for revenues. Thus it is plausible, although not always accurate, to assume that revenues will continue to flow so long as specifications are maintained. This assumption in turn allows costs to be reduced safely. In service environments like GFS, by contrast, it is difficult to fix specifications for processes like complaint resolution because the customer's perception of the adequacy of the process, rather than physical specifications of a product, determines its revenue consequences. The hazards of taking cost reductions without considering their revenue consequences in service environments is illustrated by the initial outcome of the ABC project: the ABC team initially classified zero-defect team leadership as unnecessary and problem resolution as overperformed because the frequency of inquiries and complaints had decreased sharply. But the team changed its mind in light of data showing the impact of problem resolution expenditures on customer satisfaction and attrition.

Using ABPA to find revenue drivers

At this point, it is worthwhile to return to figure 4.1 and to consider the implications of activity-based costing for the problem of separating cost drivers from revenue drivers. As we have just seen, activity-based costing can go awry when costs dominate and the revenue implications of activities are ignored. But activity-based costing is not the culprit. The culprit is a narrow view of the capabilities of activity-based costing. In fact, ABC is capable of distinguishing cost drivers from revenue drivers if three conditions are met: (1) if the costs of activities are known, (2) if the revenues generated by each customer are known, and (3) if the activities performed for each customer are also known. The first condition, of course, is met by ABC, which estimates activity costs. The second condition depends on the firm – firms that cultivate long-term customer relationships will often track revenues for individual customers, whereas firms engaging in one-off transactions or selling in mass markets generally will not. The third condition obtains far less frequently.

Few firms, retail firms especially, will track the activities performed for individual customers due to the systems requirements imposed by having to monitor the frequency with which many different kinds of activities are performed for many thousands of customers. In the past, only firms having close relationships with relatively small numbers of customers, such as the Swedish manufacturer of heating wire Kanthal, have tracked activities performed for individual customers in order to determine which customers are profitable and which are not.[12] ABPA models identifying profitable products and services tell your people what to sell (and, in some instances, what to provide without charge), but they require systems capable of tracking all of your customers' transactions with the firm and the costs of these transactions. Tracking the frequency of activities performed for large numbers of customers, it turns out, is essential if the revenue consequences of activities are to be estimated as in panel (b) of figure 4.1. In that figure, the frequencies with which activities are performed for the customer both drive customer profitability and enter into the calculation of customer profitability. Customer profitability is revenues less activity costs, the latter calculated as the frequency times the unit cost of activities performed for each customer.

The ABC team in Country A did not initially imagine that activity-based costing would help solve the problem of linking activities with revenues. But after several brainstorming sessions, the team rediscovered the system used to estimate customer profitability three years earlier and maintained, perhaps inadvertently, since. Although the cost estimates generated by this system were crude, the system was capable of tracking several hundred categories of customer transactions, attaching costs to these transactions, and comparing transaction costs to customer net revenue for retail customers. Once these capabilities were brought to management's attention, the system was upgraded in two key respects. First, it was expanded from 200 types of customer transactions capturing 28 percent of total expenditures to more than 700 types of transactions capturing nearly 60 percent of total expenditures. Second, it was converted from a batch system producing monthly reports to a production system tracking customer transactions in real time. Most importantly for our purposes, a new activity-based costing project aimed at estimating the costs of customer transactions – not all activities – was initiated. These cost estimates were extremely fine-grained. Customer transactions were first broken down into customer-initiated (front-office) and support (back-office) transactions. Then direct (operational) and indirect (mainly supervisory) activities supporting these transactions were identified. Next, the costs of these activities were established by determining employees' time allocation and the current utilization of premises and technology. Finally, activity costs were reported in three categories: short-term variable costs sensitive to the volume of customer transactions (e.g., front-line employees), long-term variable costs somewhat sensitive to the volume of transactions (e.g., supervision), and capacity costs that would be incurred if the volume of transactions required expanded premises or new equipment.[13]

Some outstanding issues

Some outstanding issues should be raised at this point. Two are quite practical. Can non-financial measures, satisfaction and courtesy measures especially, be folded into ABPA? And can any measurement system as complex as ABPA be sustained in dynamic business environments? A third issue takes us back to the core issues of this book: in the end, does ABPA resolve some of the endemic issues surrounding performance measurement?

Can non-financial measures be folded into ABPA?

An important question is whether the non-financial measures can be folded into ABPA. There is no experience in folding non-financial measures into ABPA, but, in principle, it can be done whenever data on individual customers are available. This turns out not to be a simple matter.

Consider, first, the transaction frequency and transaction cost side of ABPA. What is critical for the customer may be not whether the transaction occurred but whether the transaction was courteous – did the representative smile and say thank you? In principle, employee courtesy could be tracked transaction by transaction so that customer revenues could be estimated as a function of the frequency *and* courtesy of transactions. As a practical matter, of course, it is difficult to track courtesy transaction by transaction – the monitoring costs and intrusiveness are too high for both employer and employee. Moreover, what is considered courteous in some cultures or subcultures may not be in others. To illustrate: speed may be valued over politeness in parts of Asia, even to the point of omitting "thank you" when ending conversations. In Latin America, by contrast, politeness takes precedence over speed, and conversations are often protracted.[14]

Consider, next, the outcome side of ABPA. So far, I have empha-
sized that the critical outcomes are revenues less costs. Even so, the
ABPA framework can be adapted to pinpoint the transactions driving
certain non-financial outcomes and hence the costs of improving these
outcomes. For example, an ABPA-like approach could be used to understand the causes of customer retention, which can easily be tracked
customer by customer. Retention rates could easily be estimated as a
function of customer transactions and transaction costs, since all of the
needed data are available in ABPA. This would be a cost-of-retention
study rather than ABPA, but the logic parallels ABPA. Conceivably, an
ABPA-like approach could be used to pinpoint the transactions driving customer satisfaction and hence the cost of customer satisfaction.
I would welcome the opportunity to apply an ABPA-like framework
to customer satisfaction, but doing so would require much larger sam-
pling factions than are typical in customer-satisfaction surveys.[15]

Thus, while ABPA is not in principle antagonistic to non-financial
measurement, ABPA is useful only where non-financial measures are
available for individual customers. Customer retention (and even customer acquisition) data are generally available for individual customers, and it is conceivable that customer satisfaction could be
measured customer by customer as well – the obstacle is the cost of collecting these data. Data on customer satisfaction, and, more pointedly,
customer satisfaction with individual transactions, are more difficult
to obtain due to high cost and inconvenience. The same limitation
applies to measures of operational and human resources performance
that could be, but as a practical matter are not, mapped on to individual
customers – for example the speed with which transactions occur could
easily be built into ABPA models provided such data were available and
showed substantial variation from customer to customer.

Who bears the cost of inefficiency?

Activity-based costing in the context of ABPA raises the question of
who bears the costs of inefficiency. ABC is principally a costing tool: it
is normally used to identify costs and either reduce or eliminate those
which are unnecessary. When doing ABC, it is not unusual to discover that unit costs vary substantially within a firm. Indeed, the larger
the firm and the more diverse its businesses, the greater the variation
in costs across its units. From the perspective of costing, variation is

helpful because it pinpoints outliers where costs can be reduced easily. From the perspective of customer profitability or ABPA, however, this variation poses the question of whether customers should bear the cost of inefficiency. To illustrate: suppose customers A and B write three checks a month, but the cost of processing checks at A's branch is higher than at B's branch. Although A is in fact less profitable than B, should A, who is identical to B in all other respects, be treated in ABPA as less profitable than B because his account is domiciled at a high-cost branch? In other words, will A have to pay the price of his branch's inefficiency? I think the answer is no because customers A and B present identical opportunities and risks to the firm. This then means that the ABC cost estimates will have to be standardized across the firm before they can be entered into ABPA. The standard cost of an activity will not be its highest cost within the firm, it may be in the vicinity of the average cost, and it may be well above the lowest cost if the lowest cost is the result of unusual circumstances such as fully amortized premises and equipment.

Can ABPA be sustained?

Can any system as complex as ABPA be sustained in dynamic environments? One source of the complexity of ABPA is its dependence on activity-based costing, which is itself arduous and must be updated periodically as shifts in the organization and its technology occur. Another source of complexity lies in the need for systems capable of tracking customer transactions in real time. Still another layer of complexity lies in the models used to estimate the impact of transactions and products on revenues, which involve many variables and uncertain lags.

To the skeptics, I offer four observations. First, ABC, which is the foundation of ABPA, is admittedly complicated, but it is not necessary to do full activity-based costing to understand order-of-magnitude differences in costs, such as the difference between the cost of balance inquiries handled by automated voice response units and inquiries handled by platform officers.

Second, systems capable of tracking customer transactions in real time are already in place in many large firms. ABPA requires three kinds of data: the costs of activities, the revenues generated by each customer, and the activities performed for each customer. ABC generates activity costs; most relationship-based businesses track customer revenues; and many businesses track the activities performed for their customers. ABPA tracks all three and then estimates revenues net of costs as a function of activities performed for the customer, and hence captures the direct and indirect contributions of activities to net revenues, the latter being the value of the customer relationship.

Third, in practice the models used to estimate the revenues flowing from transactions and products need not be as complicated as figures 4.3 and 4.4 suggest. It turns out, for example, that a relatively small number of transactions account for most of the costs in GFS's Country A retail business – for example nine types of teller transactions account for more than 97 percent of teller costs.

Fourth, the complexity of models estimating revenues flowing from transactions and products must be balanced against the potential pay-off of such models. In the past decade, firms have reduced costs enormously without the benefit of analytic tools capable of separating cost drivers from revenue drivers. Further cost-downs will not come as easily and will have to be more selective than at present. The virtue of ABPA is its selectivity: ABPA separates profitable from unprofitable activities, and it is capable of doing this for each customer segment. Rather than dwelling on whether ABPA models are too complex to be implemented and dismissing them for this reason, managers should ask whether simpler alternatives to ABPA-like modeling exist.

Does ABPA resolve critical measurement issues?

This chapter began by asking when cost drivers are also revenue drivers, and then showed why it is so difficult to separate the two, particularly in relationship-driven businesses with diverse customers, where the impact of specific products and services on revenue flows is unclear. Specifications often act as surrogates for revenue drivers where goods are manufactured or services can be blueprinted in advance. Where specifications do not exist, or cannot be separated from the activities needed to produce a product or service, however, it is much more difficult to separate the cost drivers from the revenue drivers, and businesses frequently go through a boom–bust cycle, first spending on customer service to attract and retain customers and then cutting costs because their cost structure is no longer competitive. ABPA is intended to modulate this cycle by moving firms more steadily in the direction of profitability.

ABPA also addresses larger issues, which were anticipated at the beginning of this book. ABPA implements the elemental conception of the firm by reducing the firm to its activities and the costs, customers, and revenues associated with them. ABPA, in other words, is a method of partitioning the firm analytically, activity by activity and customer by customer. Partitioning a firm analytically, by activities and customers, rather than organizationally following lines of authority, offers substantial advantages for performance measurement and performance improvement. You do not have to worry about rolling up non-financial measures from the bottom to the top of the organization. You do not have to worry about modeling relationships of non-financial measures to financial outcomes or combining non-financial and financial measures into an overall appraisal of performance. And you need not worry that your cost-cutting initiatives will exact an untoward toll on revenues. ABPA relieves these worries because it makes the financial consequences of what you do transparent, or as transparent as they can be made. The strength of ABPA is that it makes sense conceptually and thus promises to clean up many of the problems inherent in other approaches to performance measurement. Beyond this, as will be shown in the next chapter, ABPA promises to facilitate learning in organizations and simplifies people's compensation. But ABPA is not without limitations. The drivers of non-financial outcomes not captured for individual customers cannot be easily estimated by ABPA. Nor can ABPA estimate the revenue consequences of executive and staff activities performed on behalf of all customers.

Where ABPA does not apply: signaling commitments and values with performance measures

Performance measures can be used to signal organizational commitments and values as well as to measure current results and make inferences about future results. The commitments and values enunciated by senior managers are never to be taken lightly, but attaching performance measures to senior management commitments and values gives them much greater urgency. Whether ABPA and ABPA-like frameworks estimating the financial consequences of non-financial performance are likely to prove useful when performance measures are intended to signal commitments and values beyond short-term financial targets requires consideration.

A case in point is Alcoa. When Paul O'Neill, the US Treasury Secretary at the time of writing, became CEO of Alcoa in 1987, the company took several dramatic steps to change its culture, its way of doing business. Among the most important was a commitment to an injury-free workplace. Alcoa's management set a target of a 50 percent reduction in serious injuries and lost workdays within five years.[16] Here is Michael Lewis's account of why O'Neill made safety a top priority for Alcoa:

> On his first day, [O'Neill] told Alcoa's executives that they weren't going to talk people into buying more aluminum and that they weren't able to raise prices, so the only way to improve the company's fortunes was to lower its costs. And the only way to do that was with the cooperation of Alcoa's workers. And the only way to get that was to show them that you actually cared about them. And the only to do that was actually to care for them. And the way to do that was to establish, as the first priority of Alcoa, the elimination of all job-related injuries. Any executive who didn't make worker safety his personal fetish – a higher priority than profits – would be fired.[17]

O'Neill followed his words with actions. In July 1996, the president of Alcoa Fujikura Ltd., a subsidiary with plants in the Acuna region of Mexico, was fired for failing to report three accidents where workers were exposed to carbon monoxide and butane gas. In an email circulated throughout the company O'Neill wrote, "Some of you may think my decision is an unduly harsh response for a lapse in communication. I felt constrained to make it *because of the effect of these matters on our values and the possible misperception that there can be tradeoffs in these areas*" (italics added).[18]

"The possible misperception that there can be tradeoffs" is the critical phrase. O'Neill's implicit model, keeping in mind "the misperception that there can be tradeoffs," is roughly as sketched in figure 4.6. Figure 4.6 seems quite straightforward. But it is less straightforward than it seems. What is missing is a comparison of the costs of making safety a fetish and eliminating job-related injuries, on the one hand, with the cost savings realized as a consequence of eliminating injuries, showing workers that management cares, and eliciting higher levels of worker cooperation, on the other. There are good reasons for avoiding such cost–benefit comparisons. One reason lies in people's values:

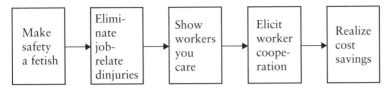

Figure 4.6 Business model of the injury-free workplace

for many, safety cannot be reduced to dollars and cents; eliminating injuries is the right thing to do regardless of what it costs or the impact on productivity and overall costs. Another reason is purely pragmatic: it may be impossible, as a practical matter, to connect reduction of job-related injuries with improved levels of cooperation and cost savings. But there may be subtler and potentially more important managerial reasons for avoiding comparisons of the cost of safety with its benefits to the corporate bottom line: if it is communicated that worker safety is valued for its contribution to the bottom line rather than for its contribution to workers' well-being, then workers will question whether management really cares and cooperation and cost savings will suffer. In other words, using ABPA and ABPA-like frameworks to compare the costs and cost savings of worker safety undermines the credibility of safety measures as signals that management cares about workers.

None of this is news to organizational sociologists, who have argued for years that the most effective managers mobilize their people by enunciating and enforcing values distinctive to the organization, sometimes called infusing the organization with value.[19] For present purposes, it is important to recognize that many everyday performance measures, for example, customer satisfaction and employee satisfaction, can used for purely instrumental purposes, that is, to track customer and employee sentiment as a precursor of the bottom line. The same measures, however, can be used as signals communicating that the organization is committed to and values its customers and its people. If the former, then comparing the costs of satisfying customers and employees with the bottom-line revenues resulting from satisfaction poses no particular issues. But if the latter, then cost–benefit calculations will undermine the credibility of these measures as signals of the organization's intent and hence the long-run benefits of having these measures.

The bottom line

Here, in summary form, are some of the key points to be taken away from this chapter:

- The problem of separating cost drivers from revenue drivers is fundamental to performance measurement. Removing costs and cost drivers without knowledge of their consequences for revenues can lead to untoward results.
- Where revenue drivers are known or can be assumed, e.g. where products are manufactured to physical specifications known to add value or where service specifications are known to add value because customer preferences are homogeneous, productivity and hence performance can be improved by removing cost while holding specifications constant.
- Where revenue drivers are not known or cannot be assumed, e.g. where neither product nor service specifications adding value for customers are known, revenue drivers must be separated from cost drivers analytically in order to manage costs effectively.
- A method called activity-based profitability analysis or ABPA, which adds a revenue component to activity-based costing, can help separate cost drivers from revenue drivers analytically by revealing the revenue consequences of activities. ABPA may be most helpful in settings where the transactions and products adding value for customers in excess of their cost is not known.
- An ABPA-like framework can also be used to estimate the drivers of non-financial outcomes like customer retention. What is critical is the measurement of such outcomes customer by customer.
- ABPA and ABPA-like frameworks may not be appropriate where performance measures are intended to communicate commitments and values of the organization rather than to gauge precursors of future cash flows.

5 | *Learning from ABPA*

T HIS chapter is about using ABPA. ABPA can help firms and their people learn about the drivers of bottom-line results. Once the learning process initiated by ABPA is in place, however, fairly simple bottom-line measures can be used to appraise and compensate people's performance. Thus, under ABPA, the measures used to improve performance and the measures used to appraise and compensate people's contributions to performance will be different. In complex service firms, the former will consist of transaction-by-transaction cost and profitability measures, whereas the latter will consist of bottom-line measures of customer profitability. What is significant about ABPA is that it yields both the fine-grained cost and profitability measures needed to improve performance and bottom-line measures that can be cascaded further into the organization than conventional financial measures.

There are many potential drivers of any firm's bottom-line performance. Fine-grained measurement is needed to quantify the impact of these potential drivers on financial performance, to identify the most critical drivers, and to move these drivers in a direction that promotes profitability.[1] ABPA is well suited for these purposes because it attaches cost and profitability estimates to the activities and transactions performed by the firm. At the same time, measures that are simpler and coarser than those provided by ABPA are needed to appraise and compensate people's performance. Whether performance is appraised relative to peers or against a fixed target, the compensation decisions that ultimately result are one-dimensional. People are ranked, and some are paid more than others. The fewer and hence coarser the measures, the easier it is to rank and pay people. It seems, then, that firms need both fine-grained measures to improve performance and coarse-grained measures to appraise and compensate performance. The need for both kinds of measures occurs at all levels of the organization. It is not simply a matter of applying fine-grained measures at the bottom and coarse-grained measures at the top.

When pressed, economists will express no clear preference between fine- and coarse-grained measures. Their models suggest that, ideally, the drivers of firm performance should also drive performance appraisals and compensation – in other words, measurement should be fine grained throughout. But their observations reveal that, in practice, compensation schemes are far simpler and rely on many fewer measures than their models suggest they should. As David Kreps puts it, "The models we analyzed suggested that optimal incentive schemes will in general be very complex, depending on the very fine structure of the environment. This is not a prediction that is verified empirically; incentive schemes in practice are usually quite simple." The explanation, according to Kreps, is that people will manipulate fine-grained incentive schemes, whereas their ability to manipulate coarser measures, especially bottom-line financial results, is limited.[2] The analysis of the balanced scorecard in chapter 3 buttresses Kreps' view. Any formula that assigns fixed weights to measures invites gaming of the formula – as we saw in chapter 3, people quickly discovered how to earn large bonuses without delivering bottom-line financial results. But without a formula, compensation becomes subjective, which has pitfalls as well. In chapter 3 we also saw that attempts to weight multiple financial and non-financial measures subjectively proved unwieldy and time-consuming, and, perhaps worse, ultimately led to imbalance where financial measures dominated.

To establish that ABPA provides a basis for learning, I will first show that measurement systems used for process improvement are, like ABPA, extremely fine grained and very demanding in use, much different from the simplicity that is sought when compensating people and also much different from the coarser measures populating corporate scorecards. I will then review how the measures generated by ABPA can contribute to learning and how, at the same time, they can be used to measure people's contributions to the performance of the organization and to compensate their contributions. Finally, I will explore the advantages and disadvantages of ABPA compared to the two dominant approaches to performance measurement: financial measurement, which focuses on bottom-line results and value for the shareholder, and the balanced scorecard, which measures non-financial drivers and financial results simultaneously. While ABPA has many advantages, it is not easy to implement. This raises the question of when firms will forgo ease of implementation for the advantages ABPA offers and when they will not.

This chapter, then, is not a "how to do it" manual for users of ABPA. Not enough is known about ABPA to write confidently about "how to do it." Rather, it presents a viewpoint on how ABPA should be used and argues that ABPA-like measurement systems can be of substantial benefit to firms whose bottom-line performance depends on how well they manage complex customer relationships.

How fine-grained measurement aids organizational learning

Two well-known cases illustrate how fine-grained measurement contributes to learning and process improvement in firms. One case is automobile assembly, where the system at Toyota remains the benchmark but in which other manufacturers have made large strides as well. The other is software development, where the Carnegie-Mellon Software Engineering Institute's capability-maturity model has become the standard used to appraise the quality of the development process.

Automobile assembly

Central to the Toyota production system are detailed job specifications. Consider the installation of a Camry front seat:

[There are] seven tasks, all of which are expected to be completed in 55 seconds as the car moves forward at a fixed speed through a worker's zone. If the production worker finds himself doing task 6 (installing the rear seat-bolts) before task 4 (installing the front seat-bolts), then the job is actually being done differently than it was designed to be done, indicating that something must be wrong. Similarly, if after 40 seconds the worker is still on task 4, which should have been completed after 31 seconds, then something, too, is amiss. To make problem detection even simpler, the length of the floor in each work area is marked in tenths. So if the worker is passing the sixth of the ten floor marks (that is, if he is 33 seconds into the cycle) and is still on task 4, then he and his team leader know that he has fallen behind. Since the deviation is immediately apparent, worker and supervisor can move to correct the problem right away and then determine how to change the specifications or retrain the worker...[3]

Note that job specifications in the Toyota production system, although detailed, are not fixed. Quite the opposite – the specifications are regarded as hypotheses to be tested: the task either can or cannot be completed to specifications within the allotted time, and specifications either can or cannot be improved so that the time required to complete the task can be reduced.

The Toyota production system, of course, involves much more than fine-grained measurement embodied in job specifications. It involves delegating the task of improvement to workers themselves. Workers become, in effect, their own production engineers. Methods and standards are determined by work teams, workers time their own jobs, compare alternative procedures to determine the most efficient one, and propose new procedures.[4]

Fine-grained measurement is also used in Honda assembly plants, although in a slightly different way. Honda's quality process involves unusually rich data, including a great deal of "market-in" or customer data. Problems are not categorized. Instead, workers are asked to "see the actual part in the actual situation" as well as to listen to customers. The benefits of fine-grained measurement at Honda are earlier problem detection and speedier problem resolution than at GM or Ford.[5]

By contrast to Toyota and Honda, approaches to job design eschewing fine-grained measurement have been largely unsuccessful in the automobile industry. Volvo's Uddevalla plant, which was closed in 1992, delegated job design to self-managed work teams. While team members were highly trained, they had very little guidance as to how to measure their performance and redesign tasks to reduce cycle times. The only performance measures available to Uddevalla workers were aggregate results based on two-hour work cycles. Absent fine-grained measurement, Uddevalla workers were either unable or unwilling to track their performance task by task. As a consequence, work cycles at Uddevalla remained at two hours (compared to one minute at Toyota), and Uddevalla's overall productivity lagged behind industry standards. Whether a distant management or recalcitrant work teams are to blame for the absence of fine-grained measurement at Uddevalla is immaterial. What is important is that Uddevalla workers did not achieve world-class productivity with only coarse measures available to them.

Software development

A standard set of metrics for assessing the quality of software development processes has been used worldwide since 1987. These metrics, known as the capability-maturity model (CMM), are maintained by the Software Engineering Institute of Carnegie Mellon University.[6] CMM measures are intended to guide incremental improvement in software development. Five stages of development are posited in the CMM model,[7] and several key process attributes (KPAs) are specified for each stage beyond the initial one.[8] The measures of process attributes are extremely detailed – the 1994 CMM questionnaire required 42 pages to cover 129 items. The hypothesis underlying CMM is that effective practices must be built on one another in logical progression rather than adopted scattershot. Software developers participate voluntarily in the CMM assessment program in order to gauge their rate of improvement. More than 6000 projects have been appraised so far. The Software Engineering Institute, in turn, releases reports on the current status and trends in software development. The most recent report finds, for example, that software engineering continues to shift toward higher maturity levels; that maturity levels remain incrementally higher overseas compared to in the USA; and that software development processes are more advanced in large than in small firms.[9]

Even though the CMM metrics are qualitative, feedback from the appraisal process appears to aid organizational learning. For example, software developers working under contract to the US Air Force were more likely to meet schedules and stay within budgets as they moved from lower to higher levels of maturity.[10] Similarly, as maturity levels improved in a software development laboratory of a Fortune 100 company, software quality improved also (although costs remain unchanged).[11] Cross-sectionally, self-reported organizational performance measured by product quality, customer satisfaction, productivity, and morale appears to be higher at higher levels of maturity. And case studies reveal improvements in productivity, time to market, and defect rates as a result of participation in the CMM process.[12]

Generalizing beyond two cases

I use automobile assembly and software development to illustrate an important point: extremely fine-grained measurement is the norm where learning and process improvement are sought *but performance is neither appraised nor compensated.* Fine-grained measurement contributes to learning because it specifies the current state of the system. You must know what you are doing before you can improve what you are doing. Fine-grained measurement also helps specify the actions that must be taken to achieve the desired improvement in the system. In automobile assembly, precise specifications for work sequences in conjunction with fine-grained measurement of workers' performance in their sequences suggest opportunities to rethink sequences, retrain workers, or both. In software development, fine-grained measurement identifies the current stage of development processes, and hence the steps that should be taken to move these processes to their next stage.

In both automobile assembly and software development, then, fine-grained measures describe and measure improvement in processes but are not used to appraise and compensate people's performance. This raises two questions: (1) are different kinds of measures needed to describe and improve performance on the one hand, and appraise and compensate performance on the other; and (2) can a single measurement system combine both kinds of measures? Somewhat fortuitously, ABPA captures both the fine-grained measures that describe and improve performance and coarser measures that can be used to appraise and compensate people.

Learning from ABPA

Can firms learn from ABPA-like fine-grained financial measurement as they have learned from fine-grained process measurement? I believe they can, but this is not obvious. There has been considerable experience with fine-grained costing, for example activity-based costing, but fine-grained revenue accounting is novel. Moreover, the action implications of ABPA revenue estimates do not seem obvious, whereas the action implications of measures showing assembly-line downtime or the maturity of software development processes seem to be. It turns out, however, that a fairly simple framework transforms ABPA results into action imperatives.

The screen in front of the banker

ABPA computer screens contain a great deal of customer information. The opening window for each customer has identifying information, a list of current accounts, and a traffic signal in the upper left corner. A red light indicates that the customer has been unprofitable for three months; a yellow light indicates marginal profitability; and a green light indicates profitability. Customer net revenue (CNR) for the last three months, gross revenues less the cost of funds, is also shown on the opening screen. Subsequent screens display transactions by frequency, ABC unit transaction costs, and the ABPA estimate of the contribution of each type of transaction to customer profitability. The ordering of transaction screens is sensitive to who the viewer is. Tellers, for example, first see a list of deposit, withdrawal, and balance inquiry transactions by channel, which allows them to compare costs and estimated profits from teller, ATM, and telephone transactions. The initial teller screens are shown in figure 5.1. The upper screen in figure 5.1 conveys the following information to the teller: the Jones household maintains large balances, revenue from which places it in segment G, the second highest customer segment (the highest segment is H). The Jones household is consistently profitable over the last quarter, and hence the bright green signal (placed beneath the yellow and red signals, which are dimmed in the upper portion of figure 5.1). The implicit message conveyed by the initial screen is: this is a profitable customer. Be especially courteous and helpful. The second screen contains information about the types of transactions most frequently encountered at the teller window. In the case of the Jones household, most of these transactions are of little consequence for their profitability given the large balances in their accounts. However, there have been seven balance inquiries in the last quarter, three to tellers and four to customer representatives at the GFS call center (since the Jones household is consistently profitable, their phone calls are automatically directed to customer representatives rather than automated voice response units). Teller balance inquiries are generally unprofitable for customers in the Joneses' segment, but balance inquiries made to the GFS call center are generally profitable because the customer representatives taking the calls are, unlike tellers, experienced salespeople. The second screen, then, prompts the teller to encourage the Joneses to check their balances frequently by phone.

Officers first see lists of non-financial transactions, which include balance inquiries, other types of inquiries, complaints, automatic payment and stop-payment orders, conversations about financial products whether or not a sale resulted, conversations about financial planning, and the like. Subsequent officer screens display product sales by channel – some products sold within branches are also available by telephone and through an outside sales force, again allowing the

Primary account checking   123456-78
Balance: $23,456.78

Joe and Mary Jones
333 4th Street
Anywhere, MS 67890

CNR 1-1-00 – 3-31-00: $238.50
Segment: G

Additional account information:

. . . .

Primary account 123456-78

	#	ABC Unit Cost	APBA Unit Revenue	Contribution to Customer Profitability
Deposit teller	3	1.40	1.28	−0.36
Deposit ATM	2	0.80	0.94	0.28
Deposit mail	0	0.95	0.65	0.00
Deposit electronic	0	0.35	1.55	0.00
Withdrawal teller	1	0.90	−0.25	−0.65
Withdrawal ATM	3	0.40	0.22	0.54
Balance inquiry teller	3	1.65	−0.60	−3.15
Balance inquiry call ctr	4	1.50	4.80	13.20
Balance inquiry AVR	0	0.15	0.00	0.00

Figure 5.1 ABPA screens

profitability of channels to be compared. The ABPA profitability estimates, but not ABC costs, of transactions are sensitive to customer segment, the latter a function of CNR, and whether the customer is a household or business or professional establishment.

Action and learning under ABPA

Whether ABPA will aid organizational learning is far more important than the details of its design. The contribution of ABPA to learning will depend on several factors: whether the action implications of transaction-by-transaction profitability data and customer profitability data are communicated successfully and whether people will, in fact, take action once they understand these implications; whether people will learn from their actions; and whether ABPA is a one-time event, in which case the opportunities for learning are limited, or whether it is a sustained process, in which case learning opportunities will abound.

Action implications
Though unfamiliar, the potential action implications of ABPA are vast. The easiest way to begin understanding these action implications is by examining the typical relationship of customer net revenue to customer profitability in retail banking. In figure 5.2 where customers are arrayed

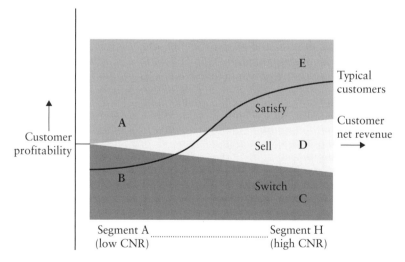

Figure 5.2 Action implications of ABPA

by CNR and profitability, this relationship is sketched by a line resembling a logistic curve.[13] Generally, the higher the CNR, the higher the customer profitability. However, the relationship is not perfect. While many low CNR customers (e.g. customer B) are unprofitable, some (e.g. customer A) are profitable. And while many high CNR (e.g. customer E) are highly profitable, some (e.g. customer D) are marginally profitable, while still others (e.g. customer C) are unprofitable.

Figure 5.2 also displays three bands corresponding to the color of the traffic signal on the opening ABPA screen. The green (upper) band consists of customers who are consistently profitable; the yellow (central) band, which is in fact a wedge, consists of marginally profitable customers; and the red (lower) band consists of unprofitable customers. An action imperative is attached to each of these bands. For the green band, the imperative is *satisfy*: meet and, if possible, exceed the customer's expectations. For the yellow band, the imperative is *sell*: offer profitable products and services to the customer. For the red band, the imperative is *switch*: move the customer to less costly transactions if possible, raise prices if necessary, or terminate the relationship if it remains unprofitable. Note that the yellow band grows in height from left to right in figure 5.2. This occurs because transactions become more profitable and sales opportunities more attractive in higher CNR segments.

The two dimensions of figure 5.2 are customer net revenue and customer profitability, the latter computed as CNR minus the cost of all activities performed for the customer. ABPA estimates of transaction profitability do not enter into the construction of figure 5.2. However, pinpointing specific actions likely to satisfy, sell, or switch customers requires ABPA profitability estimates and ABC costs. Consider again hypothetical customers A, B, C, D, and E, keeping in mind that all of the information contained in these vignettes is generated by ABPA:

- Customer A's screen shows a green light but very few transactions: she pays a monthly fee to maintain checking privileges and a line of credit, and makes one deposit and writes five checks in a typical month. Since ABPA estimates indicate that few if any transactions will be profitable in customer A's segment, the best strategy is satisfy: meet customer A's requirements but do not attempt to sell her new products and services.

- Customer B's screen shows a red light: he, like customer A, pays a monthly fee to maintain checking privileges and a line of credit. Unlike customer A, however, customer B writes twenty checks a month, some for cash, and also phones or visits his branch three times a week to inquire about his checking balance (interest rates are quite high, making loans to cover overdrafts expensive). Since few transactions are profitable in customer B's segment, the best strategy for the bank is to switch customer B: encourage him to use ATMs rather than tellers for balance inquiries and cash withdrawals, and route his phone calls to an automated voice response unit rather than an operator. If customer B fails to switch his transactions to less expensive channels, then the bank should consider terminating the relationship.
- Customer C's screen shows a red light even though he generates a great deal of revenue for the bank and is in the top customer segment. Customer C operates a retail business – a chain of pharmacies – and maintains multiple business and household relationships with the bank: checking, personal loans, business loans, both personal and business insurance, and investments. Customer C is nonetheless unprofitable because he deposits several hundred customer checks daily. Although ABPA estimates show that many transactions in customer C's segment are likely to be profitable, the cost of processing the number of checks deposited by customer C far exceeds the profitability of any new products or services customer C might acquire. Thus, the best strategy is to switch customer C: either price his checking account by transaction volume, or, should customer C not accept repricing, terminate the relationship.
- Customer D's screen shows a yellow light. Customer D is a professional and is also in the top customer segment. Like customer C, customer D maintains multiple relationships with the bank. Unlike customer C, he has a normal level of activity in his checking account, but he visits his branch more often than customer C and makes much greater use of services provided without charge. Customer D, for example, meets with an officer twice a month to review his investments; he has asked for his statements and checkbooks to be delivered by courier because he feels it is unsafe to carry them and finds the mail service unreliable; and he asks the bank to pay his bills when he travels, which he does often. As a consequence, customer D is only marginally profitable. Since ABPA estimates indicate that several products might still be sold profitably to customer D, the best

strategy is sell: whenever customer D is in the bank, offer him one of these products.
- Little need be said about customer E. She is so profitable that the bank need only strive to exceed her expectations at all times.

There is another way to understand the impact of these action imperatives. Consider the opportunities forgone absent ABPA: customer B would continue to use expensive channels and hence remain unprofitable; customer C would continue to deposit hundreds of checks without charge and hence remain unprofitable; and customer D would not be the target of an aggressive sales effort, and hence remain marginally profitable.

Learning from action

Once ABPA is initially in place, the challenge is to motivate people to take action, learn from their actions, and then take further action aimed at improving customer profitability. The success of this action–learning–action cycle depends on whether people can be motivated to behave like scientists, that is to test hypotheses about the impact of their actions on customer profitability, and then to behave like business people, that is to act on what they have learned in order to maximize customer profitability. People will be motivated to play both roles if they can see how both contribute to bottom-line results.

The steps in the ABPA action–learning–action cycle are as follows:

- Step 1: Take action based on the customer's position in the revenue-profitability array. Satisfy, sell, or switch customers depending on whether they fall in the green, yellow, or red band.
- Step 2: Act like a scientist. For each segment, ask whether total customer profitability improved as the result of the actions you took. This is relatively easy. All that is needed is total CNR, ABC estimates of transaction costs, and transaction frequencies for customers in each segment. Figure 5.3 illustrates the expected impact of your action on CNR and customer profitability: the line describing the relationship of CNR to profitability for typical customers will shift somewhat to the left, indicating higher revenues, and upward, indicating higher profitability.
- Step 3: Act like a scientist again. Ask which of your actions affected the profitability of individual customers. This is more complicated

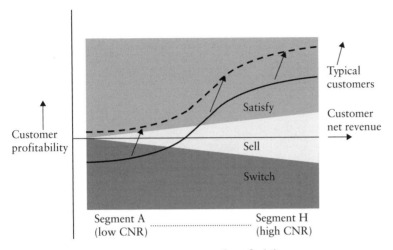

Figure 5.3 Improve customer revenues and profitability

than asking whether total customer profitability improved, since you must estimate the impact of *changes* in the frequency of each kind of transaction on subsequent *changes* in customer profitability, again segment by segment. But the real learning occurs at this point. Going forward, you will have a much better understanding of why your actions produced the result they did. Did switching customers to less costly transactions improve profitability, or did it have the reverse effect because of unforeseen consequences, for example lost sales opportunities when balance inquiries were moved to the automated voice response unit? Did selling profitable products improve profitability, or were there again unforeseen consequences, for example losing customers who then began to comparison shop?

- Step 4: Recalibrate the green, yellow, and red bands. As customer profitability improves, the bands suggesting action imperatives will move upward as illustrated in figure 5.4. The upward shift signals higher profitability targets for customers in all segments. It also signals greater willingness to switch (and possibly terminate) customers who remain marginally profitable.

- Step 5: Return to step 1 and take further action based on knowledge of how your actions improved customer profitability and the recalibrated action imperatives.

These five steps, which comprise the action–learning–action cycle, should lead to continuous improvement in customer profitability. The

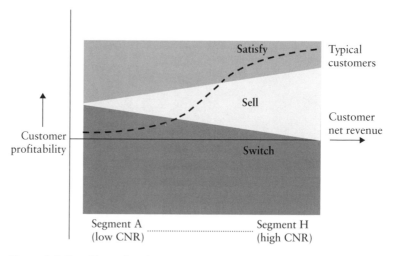

Figure 5.4 Recalibrate bands

logic of these steps is, in fact, the logic of continuous improvement: understand the process, improve the process, revise targets upward, and then improve the process further. All that is distinctive about the action–learning–action cycle in this instance is its dependence on a human element not completely under the control of the organization: rather than seeking to improve operational performance, ABPA seeks to improve profitability, which is ultimately under the control of *the customer*, who chooses whether to supply revenues and profits to the firm.

Sustaining learning

Sustained learning requires managers to revisit and recalibrate activity costs, transaction-by-transaction profitability, and customer profitability targets on an ongoing basis. ABPA, in other words, will contribute little to learning if it is viewed as a one-time intervention. To be sure, ABPA can be installed by consultants. But its benefits will not be realized unless managers struggle with the issues of connecting costs with revenue consequences, improving their understanding of connections between costs and revenues with experience, and revising cost and revenue estimates as the organization improves its performance. Thus, while data collection for ABPA can readily be automated, the learning process cannot be. Sustained learning from ABPA requires sustained managerial attention.

Compensating people under ABPA

Under ABPA, people can easily be compensated for customer profitability. ABPA is not congenial to compensating people for performance on aggregate non-financial performance measures, for example growth in the customer base. Nor is ABPA congenial to compensating people for revenues while ignoring costs. Ideally, compensation under ABPA would be awarded for long-term customer profitability, but as a practical matter it is critical for people to perceive a close connection between their accomplishments and their pay packets. A middle ground might be to base compensation on customer profitability over the past three to six months.

There are several advantages to compensating people for customer profitability rather than for other financial measures such as profit margins or sales. One advantage, which is straightforward, is that customer profitability can be cascaded deeper into the organization than profit margins. Profit margins can be computed only at the point where revenues and expenses are joined in the organization, usually the firm as a whole or its business units. In a typical retail bank branch, profits or margins can be computed for the branch as a whole but cannot be cascaded to account managers. Customer profitability, by contrast, can be calculated for account managers (the profitability of their customers) as well as for the branch manager (the profitability of branch customers). But the advantages of compensating people for customer profitability rather than earnings go beyond this. As we have seen, ABPA identifies the drivers of customer profitability in a way that is very easy to understand: the drivers of customer profitability are customer transactions, and the impact of customer transactions on customer profitability is measured in dollars. Since the connection between the drivers of customer profitability and the customer profitability result that is sought is transparent, it is sufficient to compensate customer profitability to induce people to engage in more rather than less profitable transactions. By contrast, finding the drivers of branch profitability and quantifying their impact is more difficult, as the analysis of the balanced scorecard in chapter 4 demonstrated.

A potential objection to compensating people for customer profitability is that the latter depends on ABC cost estimates that fail to take account of fixed costs. This objection must be acknowledged, but at the same time it must also be acknowledged that reported profit

margins for retail branches often omit significant fixed *and* variable
costs. The cost of processing back-office transactions, for example, are
frequently not allocated to the branches where transactions originate.

ABPA thus presents a happy coincidence. On the one hand, ABPA
measures organizational performance at the level of activities and customer transactions. Such fine-grained measurement, as we have seen, is
conducive to learning and improvement. On the other hand, ABPA also
measures customer profitability, a bottom-line measure that captures
people's performance and can be readily tied to their compensation.
This happy coincidence must never be overlooked when weighing the
benefits of ABPA against its costs and complexity.

Financial measures and the balanced scorecard versus ABPA

At this point, it may be useful to compare financial measurement, the
balanced scorecard, and ABPA. In table 5.1, these measurement systems
are compared and evaluated on several dimensions: measures and units,
ease of implementation, learning, compensation, and assumptions.

Is ABPA advantageous?

Measures and units

Financial measures report bottom-line results for firms and business
units – the different kinds of financial measures were reviewed in chapter 1. Balanced scorecard measures include bottom-line financial results
as well as non-financial measures in several domains, usually at the level
of firms and business units[14] – the balanced scorecard was discussed
in chapter 3. ABPA measures are quite different. ABPA measures profitability at the level of customers and customer transactions. In principle, profitability could be measured at the level of activities as well.
Customer profitability is measured for individual customers, and can
be rolled up from individual customers to the top of the organization.
ABPA measures the profitability of customer transactions for customer
segments but not for individual customers. Like customer profitability, however, the profitability of customer transactions can be rolled up
from the bottom to the top of the organization. Financial and scorecard measures thus are largely top-down but do not go very far down
in the organization. ABPA measures, on the other hand, can be rolled
up from the bottom to the top of the organization.

Table 5.1 Comparison of financial measures, the balanced scorecard, and ABPA

	Measure and units	Performance drivers	Compensating people	Learning	Implementation
Financial measures only	Bottom-line results for firm and business units	Bottom-line results are sufficient to capture performance	Based on bottom-line results	No provision for learning	Bottom-line results easily measured; based on accounting data
Balanced scorecard only	Bottom-line results plus non-financial measures for firm and business units	Drivers of bottom-line results are known	In principle, based on bottom-line *and* non-financial results; in fact, bottom line often dominates	Communicates strategy: scorecard measures make business model explicit	Bottom-line results easily measured; non-financials more difficult to measure
ABPA	Customer profitability and profitability of customer transactions by segment	Drivers of bottom-line results must be discovered	Based on customer and customer transaction profitability	Understanding of drivers of customer profitability improve with experience	Relies on ABC; must track customer revenues and transactions; cannot easily track subjective states
Advantage	*ABPA*	*ABPA*	*ABPA*	*ABPA*	*Financial measures*

Financial measures are aligned with the profitability objectives of the firm but capture results only for the firm as a whole and its business units. Non-financial scorecard measures are intended to be in alignment with the profitability of the firm, but are not necessarily in alignment. Moreover, scorecard measures, like financial measures, capture results for the firm as a whole and its business units. ABPA measures of customer profitability and customer transaction profitability, by contrast, are aligned with the profitability objectives of the firm and capture results throughout the organization. Advantage: ABPA.

Performance drivers

Financial measurement assumes that bottom-line results describe the performance of the firm fully. The balanced scorecard, by contrast, assumes that measures of bottom-line results and the non-financial drivers of bottom-line results must be measured to describe the performance of the firm fully. The balanced scorecard assumes, additionally, that the non-financial drivers of the bottom line are already known. ABPA takes a further step. Like the balanced scorecard, ABPA assumes that bottom-line results and their non-financial drivers must be measured to describe the performance of the firm fully. But unlike the balanced scorecard, ABPA assumes that the drivers of bottom-line performance must be discovered through analysis of the relevant data and facilitates the discovery process by measuring the profitability – not simply the frequency – of customer transactions in real time.

In a static world, financial measures would capture the performance of the firm fully – tomorrow's results would be identical to today's. In a dynamic world, financial measures do not capture the performance of the firm fully, and non-financial drivers of bottom-line performance must be discovered rather than assumed. Advantage: ABPA.

Compensating people

Compensating people on financial measures is fairly easy. The main limitation is that connections between individual performance and overall financial results become more tenuous as one goes deeper into the organization. Compensating people for performance on scorecard measures, as we saw in chapter 3, is more challenging. This is due to the complications of combining financial and non-financial measures into an overall appraisal of performance, which can result in a reversion to purely financial measurement. Again, since scorecards typically make use of aggregate measures, connections between individual performance and scorecard measures become more tenuous the deeper one goes into the organization. Compensating people under ABPA is straightforward. People having direct customer responsibility are compensated for total customer profitability. People not having direct customer responsibility are compensated for the profitability of customer transactions for which they are responsible or that they facilitate.

Again, ABPA measures apply throughout the organization whereas financial measures and scorecard measures do not. Advantage: ABPA.

Learning

Financial measures make no provision for learning. Balanced scorecard measures, by contrast, have a learning function: they transform the business model implicit in the firm's strategy into explicit measures and connections among these measures. This roadmap of the firm's strategy, in turn, can be used to assess progress toward strategic goals and to rethink the strategy if necessary. ABPA measures have a further learning function. Not only do the ABPA measures trace initial connections between the firm's transactions with its customers and its financial results, but they also trace the trajectory of these connections over time, allowing firms to modify their customer strategies incrementally with experience.

ABPA measures thus are unique in allowing firms to move from action to learning to further action in a very short space of time. Advantage: ABPA.

Implementation

Financial measures are routinely reported by the accounting system and hence are fairly easy to implement. Implementing the balanced scorecard, as we saw, can be frustrating. Choosing non-financial measures is not easy, and measurement issues are endemic – again, recall chapter 3. Implementing ABPA poses even greater challenges, since ABPA relies on activity-based costing, which is itself costly, and the capability of firms to track customer revenues and transactions in real time, which is also costly.

Financial measurement is more economical and much better under-stood than either balanced scorecard or ABPA. Advantage: financial measures.

Ease of implementation versus quality of measurement

ABPA is superior to financial measurement and the balanced score-card with respect to the alignment of measures with the profitability objectives of the firm, its treatment of performance drivers, the way it compensates people, and opportunities for organizational learning. In short, the ABPA advantage is completeness of performance mea-surement: ABPA completes the connection between the activities per-formed by the firm and the firm's financial performance. Moreover, should these connections prove stable over time, ABPA comes close to connecting the firm's activities with its true economic performance. The advantage of financial measurement, by contrast, is ease of implemen-tation, which will be decisive in many instances. Financial measures are widely understood, most are governed by accounting conventions, and most are comparable both within and across firms. The balanced score-card falls between ABPA and financial measures on both dimensions: scorecard measures are more complete than financial measures but less complete than the measures generated by ABPA, and balanced score-cards are somewhat more difficult to implement than financial mea-sures when used to gauge progress toward strategic objectives and, as we have seen, nearly impossible to implement satisfactorily when they are used to compensate people.

Figure 5.5 arrays financial measurement, the balanced scorecard, and ABPA by quality of measurement and ease of implementation. The clear suggestion, consistent with this analysis, is that there are severe tradeoffs between ease of implementation and completeness of performance measurement. But the callouts in figure 5.5 add a new element: they suggest conditions that will cause firms to prefer ease of implementation over completeness of measurement and vice versa – in other words, where the likely payoff from ABPA falls short of its cost of implementation, and where it exceeds this cost. The conditions governing the choice of performance measures can follow from ABPA's decisive advantage (which, of course, is not costless): ABPA locates and finds opportunities for profit in differences in customer valuation of the activities performed by the firm.

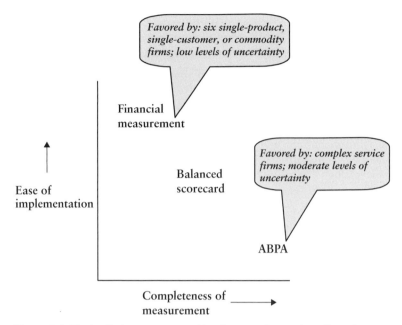

Figure 5.5 Tradeoffs between ease of implementation and quality of measurement

It follows that ABPA will be of little benefit to firms where differences in customer valuation do not exist or cannot be measured. These include firms selling to one customer (since, with a single customer, there are no differences in valuation of the firm's activities); firms selling a single product or service (since, with a single product, differences in customer valuation are reflected directly in revenues); firms selling commodity products or services (since differences in valuation will be arbitraged away by the market); and firms that provide identical products and services to all customers (since the revenue contributions of different products and services cannot be separated when they are utilized identically by customers). ABPA will have greatest benefit, then, to firms having many customers whose preferences for products and services vary and are not captured by simpler measurement systems. Complex service in industries like financial services, consulting, and possibly health care would be ideal candidates for ABPA. Interestingly, these are industries where sustained customer relationships rather than arm's-length transactions are the norm rather than the exception.

The level of uncertainty – or deterministic complexity, which has the same effect as uncertainty – posed by the environment also affects the appropriateness of ABPA. Absent uncertainty, connections between the activities, costs, customers, and revenues will be understood tacitly if not explicitly, the performance of the firm will be reflected fully in financial results, and ABPA will offer marginal benefits at best. A high level of uncertainty, by contrast, will render ABPA estimates, like all performance measures, so labile as to have little or no value looking forward. ABPA, then, will offer the greatest benefit at intermediate levels of uncertainty. In this intermediate condition, the level of uncertainty is high enough to render tacit knowledge of connections between activities, costs, customer, and revenues inadequate, but it is low enough that ABPA profitability estimates remain useful, if imperfect, indicators of the economic performance of the firm.

At the end of the day, almost all firms will retain the financial measurement systems whether or not they meet the basic requirements of performance measurement. Financial measurement is deeply embedded in most firms and the accounting profession, and firm-level financial results must be reported to shareholders and regulators. The question facing some firms, complex service firms especially, is whether they will supplement their financial measures with ABPA-like measurement systems that come much closer to meeting the basic requirements of performance measurement.

The bottom line

This chapter, as promised, was not a "how-to-do-it" manual for installing ABPA. That said, the following points should be remembered:

- Generally, fine-grained measurement is needed to improve processes, whereas coarse-grained measurement is needed to appraise and compensate people's performance.
- ABPA yields the fine-grained measures needed for improvement: the revenues and costs, and hence profitability, flowing from the activities and transactions performed by a firm. Transaction-by-transaction cost and profitability measures can be used to identify the less costly and more profitable transactions for each customer segment. Profit-maximizing strategies can be developed and tested for customers at

different levels of profitability within each segment. These strategies can be evaluated against results and improved with experience.

- ABPA yields coarse-grained measures for performance appraisal and compensation: customer profitability. People can be appraised and compensated for total customer profitability or their contributions to customer profitability.

- Compared to financial measurement and the balanced scorecard, ABPA has the advantage in most respects. The one deficiency of ABPA is ease of implementation, since ABPA depends on activity-based costing and systems capable of tracking all customer transactions, financial and non-financial, in real time.

- Firms will select ABPA to the extent that ABPA's benefits exceed its costs. These firms will typically be complex service firms with ongoing customer relationships operating at moderate levels of uncertainty.

6 | *Managing and strategizing with ABPA*

WHAT are the implications of ABPA for managing the firm and implementing its strategy? To answer this question, think of the following: in order to arrive at ABPA, we decomposed the firm into its elemental parts: activities, costs, customers, and revenues. ABPA connects these parts by linking the activities performed for the customer and the costs they incur with the revenues the customer supplies. This linkage allows us to assess whether particular activities or transactions (which are supersets of activities) or products (which are, in turn, supersets of transactions) are profitable. The profitability of an activity, transaction, or product can be assessed for the entire customer base of a firm or for segments of its customers. The profitability of customers is then the profitability of their products and transactions, that is, revenues less the costs of providing these products and transactions. Since people's performance can be appraised and rewarded against customer profitability targets, ABPA not only allows firms to identify which actions are profitable and which are unprofitable, but also allows firms to reward people for doing what is profitable and for improving the profitability of what they do. ABPA, though complicated, is thus a powerful tool for aligning people's behavior with the financial objectives of the firm.

We must now reassemble the firm from its elemental parts to make it manageable and to give it direction under ABPA. To do this, we must take two steps. The first and most important step is to locate where in the firm it is easiest to construct performance chains, that is where it is easiest to connect fine-grained measures of activities, costs, customers, and revenues. The importance of connecting fine-grained measures cannot be over-emphasized. Many firms try to assemble and connect aggregate measures of their activities, costs, customers, and revenues at or near the top of the organization. This is usually unproductive because, as we saw earlier, especially in chapter 1, aggregation is the bane of performance measurement. The second step is to shift

168

power to people who have the information needed to construct performance chains by delegating operational and strategic choices to them. Delegating strategic choices is especially important because it signals that these people are free to discover different paths to profitability or, in current language, different business models. Together, these two steps can be viewed as extending decentralization much deeper into the firm than in the past. But it is decentralization with a difference. Decisions are highly decentralized in this model: both operating and strategic decisions take place as close to the customer as possible. But operations invisible to the customer may be centralized in large units remote from the customer. The combination of decentralized decisions and centralized operations under ABPA is very different from traditional organizational designs and, interestingly, allows firms to pursue textbook low-cost and differentiation strategies simultaneously.

An organizational design for ABPA

The organizational design of firms utilizing ABPA revolves around three basic units, front-end units ("the front end") that sell and serve customers and develop customer strategies, back-end units ("the back end") that support the front end with products and services, and a systems unit that maintains information flows. The front end is specialized by customer segment: each front-end unit is responsible for one or more of these segments. The back end of the organization, by contrast, is specialized by function. Back-end functions may or may not be centralized. Where back-end functions are centralized, each back-end unit has full responsibility for a unique function and is connected to every front-end unit (e.g. a single check-clearing operation for the entire USA). Where back-end functions are decentralized, by contrast, they are divided among several units (e.g. regional check-clearing operations).

Figures 6.1–6.3 display information flows, transaction flows, and the administrative hierarchy for a firm with four front-end and three back-end units – imagine that front-end units are specialized by customer tier and geography while the back-end functions consist of operational and product units, for example check-clearing, credit analysis, and mortgages. Let's start with the transaction flows shown in figure 6.1. Most transactions are initiated by customers and flow from customers to front-end units to back-end units and then to front-end units again. To illustrate: a customer deposits a check with a teller, the check is cleared

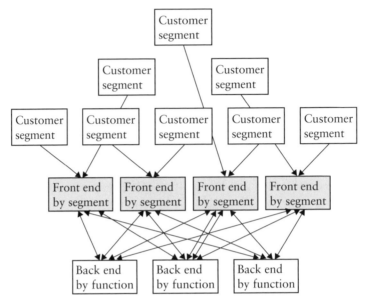

Figure 6.1 Organizational design for implementing ABPA: transaction flows (customer-initiated transactions only)

in the back office, and the teller's display then shows that the customer's account has received credit for the deposit. (Transactions initiated internally, for example, reversing clerical errors, are not considered in figures 6.1–6.3.)

Now let's turn to information flows, which are somewhat different from transaction flows. These are shown in figure 6.2. Every customer-initiated transaction results in three streams of data: customer identifiers and revenues resulting from the transaction, front-end transactions and their costs, and back-end (or support) transactions and their costs. For example, when customers deposit checks, new revenues accrue due to increased balances. But depositing a check also incurs teller costs at the front end and support costs (e.g. processing, clearing, and positing costs) at the back end of the organization. Under ABPA, the three streams of data – revenues, front-end costs, and back-end costs – are merged by front-end units, which then have a full picture of transactions, revenues, and transaction costs for each customer.

Finally, the administrative hierarchy and accountabilities of the firm are shown in figure 6.3. Administratively, the front end and the back

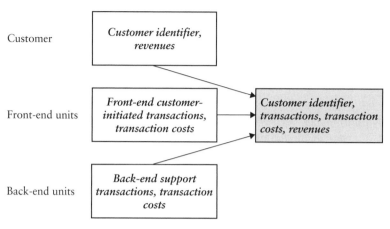

Figure 6.2 Organizational design for implementing ABPA: information flows (customer-initiated transactions only)

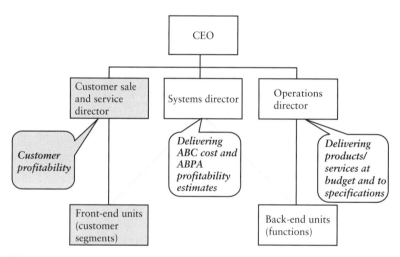

Figure 6.3 Organizational design for implementing ABPA: administrative hierarchy and accountabilities

end of the business are separated save at the pinnacle of the organization. Three line executives report to the CEO: a customer sales and service director responsible for the front end of the business, an operations director responsible for the back end, and a systems director responsible for coordinating information flows. The customer sales and service director and his reports are accountable for customer profitability, much like units in a divisionalized firm are accountable for bottom-line results. The operations director and his reports are accountable for delivering products and services at cost and to specifications set by the sales and service director and his reports – the back end of the business, in other words, is a supplier to the front end. The systems director is responsible for maintaining ABC cost and ABPA profitability estimates and assembling and delivering accurate and timely information on customers, revenues, and costs to the front-end units and cost data to back-end units.

The ABPA organization versus conventional organizational designs

The organizational design sketched in figures 6.1–6.3 departs from conventional organizational designs in several respects. Conventionally, firms are either organized by function, divisionalized, or matrixed. The organizational design in these figures, by contrast, is partly functional and partly divisionalized. Three functional units report to the CEO – front-end customer sales and service, back-end operations, and systems. The front-end customer sales and service function, however, is divisionalized internally (front-end units, though much smaller than business units in divisionalized firms, are accountable for customer profitability). The back-end operations function, by contrast, is divided by function internally (the size of functional subunits and hence the extent that functions are centralized in back-end units is driven by scale economies). Nor is this organizational design a matrix. In matrix designs, people are assigned to both business units *and* functional units and thus have dual reporting relationships. In our design, people are assigned either to front-end or to back-end units but not to both. To be sure, back-end units are accountable for delivering products and services to specifications and costs set by front-end units, but their people do not report to front-end units.

There is a further difference between conventional organizational designs and the design for firms using ABPA sketched above: the ABPA design combines functional organization with the capacity to measure profitability in much of the organization. Remove ABPA from the picture and the choices available to firms providing a large array of services to customers having different requirements are unattractive.

One choice is divisionalization and fully decentralized operations. This choice, though attractive in some settings (e.g. chain stores), is unattractive where there are substantial scale economies in back-end functions. The alternative is functional organization absent fine-grained ABPA cost and profitability metrics. This alternative is not especially attractive either, mainly because revenues (generated by front-end customer sales and service units) and costs (incurred largely but not entirely by back-end functional units) become independent events whose relationship cannot easily be understood.

To be sure, firms implementing the organizational design suggested for ABPA will not measure customer profitability throughout the organization – there are no profitability metrics for functional units at the back end of the business – and in this respect the organizational design falls somewhat short of ideal. But it does drive profitability measures much deeper into the organization, specifically to front-end customer sales and service units, account managers, and individual customers, than either functional or divisional organizational designs permit. Most importantly, the organizational design suggested for ABPA allows front-end units to connect transaction costs with the revenues resulting from customer transactions. As will be seen, the ability to make this connection allows much greater leeway for strategic choice than conventional organizational designs.

Organizational design in manufacturing versus the ABPA organization

Much of our thinking about organizational design is based on the experience of manufacturing firms. This occurs partly because manufacturing predated services, but manufacturing is also simpler than services. Whether a manufacturing firm is organized by function or divisionalized, most of its value-adding activities take place in production units at the back end of the firm or the back end of its business units. The choice between functional and divisional organization in manufacturing is thus the choice between one and several back-end production units. Services are more complicated because most of their value-adding activities are scattered across front-end units rather than concentrated in a few plants. Not only, then, will the performance measures used in manufacturing remain simpler than the ABPA-like metrics required for many service firms – recall the discussion at the beginning of chapter 4 – but it is also likely that organizational designs for manufacturing will remain simpler than organizational designs for service firms implementing ABPA.

This point can be illustrated by going back to some organizational design principles from the 1960s and then moving forward to the present. In the 1960s, an important organizing principle was isolation of the firm's "technical core" – in the case of manufacturing, its production activities – from external shocks. Two key mechanisms isolated the core from the environment: buffer inventories that smoothed input and output transactions, and multiple layers of managers who dealt with uncertainties arising externally.[1] These mechanisms are illustrated in figure 6.4.

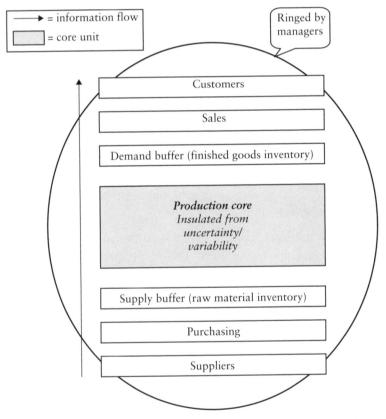

Figure 6.4 Late-1960s model of manufacturing firm: core is buffered from the environment

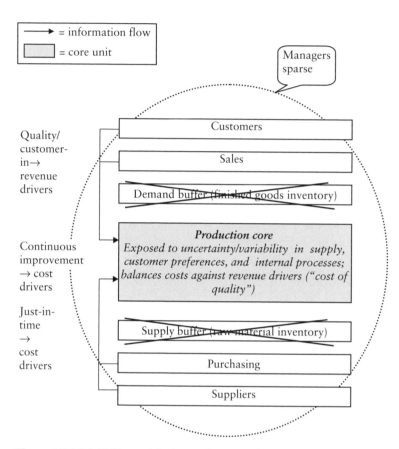

Figure 6.5 Mid-1980s model of manufacturing firm: core is exposed to environment

By the mid-1980s, the buffers and management layers surrounding the firm's "technical core" had largely disappeared, and core production activities were directly exposed to several kinds of external pressures including just-in-time delivery of materials, which reduced inventories nearly to zero; continuous improvement, which sought to reduce costs by reducing cycle times; and the quality revolution and mass customization, which drove customer preferences directly into the production process. These developments, shown in figure 6.5, forced manufacturing firms to focus on costs and revenue drivers simultaneously, just as ABPA focuses on the relationship of costs to revenues. But the overall organizational design of manufacturing firms was not altered, much in contrast to services where ABPA-like metrics capturing costs and revenues require an innovative organizational design. The difference between manufacturing and services is this: customer preferences and cost pressures can be translated into product and process specifications in manufacturing, and hence revenues can be balanced against costs or cost drivers in the core production activities of manufacturing firms. In services, by contrast, customer preferences may be idiosyncratic, many activities satisfying customer preferences take place in front-end rather than in back-end units, and the value that is added by these activities is revealed only in revenues in comparison to costs. The consequence is that front-end units capable of balancing revenues against costs are required in many service firms.

The ABPA organization and the e-commerce model

The ABPA organizational design may prove complementary to the world of electronic commerce. A distinctive characteristic of e-commerce is that it is relentlessly customer-facing. Value is produced by customer relationships rather than by tangible assets. E-commerce facilitates building customer relationships because it allows information about preferences and purchasing patterns to be accumulated inexpensively and customer by customer. The technology of the internet, of course, facilitates accumulation of this information, and this information is also accumulated because e-commerce has a molecular view of the customer:

Think of customers as individual molecules rather than mass markets, and the picture bcomes clearer. B-Webs [business webs] group their economic units to create value just as molecules cluster to form a substance. A B-Web is a collection of molecules held together by economic, personal, technological, cultural, and other forces. Customers are molecules in the B-Web. The new challenge of marketing is engineering the forces that attract and bind customers.[2]

The molecular view of the customer is taken to an extreme by web portals, e-commerce businesses providing no products or services directly but, rather, channeling customers to firms providing products and services. Not surprisingly, the dominant metrics for web portals describe relationships with their customers and business partners.

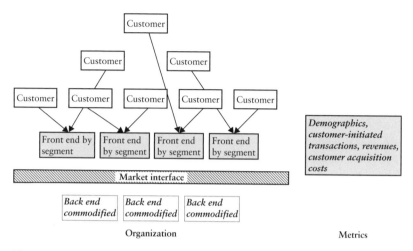

Figure 6.6 Organization and metrics of web portals

Typically, these metrics include the number of regular users, the number of page views per use, average time spent per person on the portal (its "stickiness"), the number of alliances with other businesses, and, of course, revenues. Customer metrics are more important to web portals than the more common functional metrics used throughout the internet – reliability, speed, percentage of sessions broken off – because it is easier to build customer metrics than functional metrics into portals' business models.

Web portals are thus businesses with front ends but without back ends. Figure 6.6 caricatures the organizational design of web portals – the figure does not represent the actual design of any portal. This caricature is similar to the organizational design for implementing ABPA in figure 6.1 but with two key differences. First, while the organizational design sketched in figure 6.6 shows a front end and a back end, web portals externalize the back end and manage it entirely through market interfaces with other firms rather than though an administrative hierarchy. Second, as indicated on the right of figure 6.6, web portals have no metrics capturing the activities performed for customers and the costs of these activities. This occurs mainly because the bulk of variable costs are incurred by the externalized back end – in other words, web portals' costs of performing activities directly for customers are trivial in comparison with their fixed costs and marketing costs that cannot be allocated to current customers.

The web portal model of organization has potential significance for old-economy firms for two reasons. The first concerns human resources: old-economy firms wishing to pursue ABPA-like performance measurement might consider staffing front-end units with people from e-commerce and from web portals in particular. People from e-commerce backgrounds are likely to understand customer metrics and the division between the front end and the back end of firms. They are also unlikely to be daunted by the challenge of accumulating rich customer data and delivering these data to the front end in real time. There is, of course, a potential downside: people from e-commerce and from web portals in particular are unlikely to appreciate the importance of fine-grained costing, ABC especially. The challenge is finding people versed in both customer *and* cost metrics or, alternatively, people versed in the former who can be trained in the latter. Second, going forward, old-economy firms that have adopted ABPA-like customer and cost metrics may find themselves in direct competition with customer-facing e-commerce firms having little experience in managing costs. Which of these two organizational forms will dominate – the one that joins fine-grained customer data with fine-grained cost data or the one that has rich customer data but allows market transactions to determine its costs – cannot be predicted. The argument of this book suggests that firms successfully joining fine-grained customer data with fine-grained costing will ultimately be advantaged.

ABPA as a strategic capability

ABPA, although derived from the fundamentals of performance, may extend firms' strategic capabilities in two ways.

First, ABPA opens the possibility of decentralized strategizing by supplying fine-grained cost and revenue data to decentralized customer sales and service units that make strategic choices based on these data. ABPA, in effect, asks each customer sales and service unit to model its business and improve its results by finding the drivers of customer profitability. Since these units serve different customer segments, diverse business models and hence diverse business strategies are likely to result. There are advantages and disadvantages to this outcome. The main advantage is rapid learning and adaptation, since small customer-focused units can adapt to changes in customer preferences more rapidly than larger units. The disadvantage is inconsistency, since

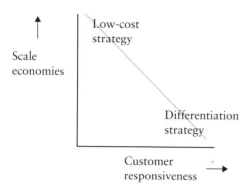

Figure 6.7 Tradeoffs between low-cost and differentiation strategies

the mix and even the pricing of products can vary across units. The possibility of decentralized strategizing raises the issue of the limits of diversification among strategies – not product or industry diversification – within a single firm.

Second, ABPA opens up the possibility that front-end and back-end units will pursue different but complementary strategies. Consider the two textbook strategies: a low-cost strategy that seeks advantage through scale economies and, ultimately, market dominance and a differentiation strategy that seeks advantage by providing specialized products and services commanding high margins. In principle, the low-cost strategy will be preferred where customer preferences are uniform and standard products and services meet customers' needs, whereas the differentiation strategy will be preferred where customer preferences are diverse and standard products and services will not meet their needs. In fact, since customers' preferences are rarely uniform, most firms are forced to think about tradeoffs between the low-cost and differentiation strategies. These tradeoffs are sketched in figure 6.7, where the placement of the low-cost strategy at the upper left indicates a combination of high scale economies and low customer responsiveness whereas the placement of the differentiation strategy at the lower right indicates the combination of low scale economies and high customer responsiveness.

Not surprisingly, some firms seek intermediate strategies combining the advantages of low cost and differentiation. A common intermediate strategy is mass customization. Mass customization adds specialized features to products built from common components or on

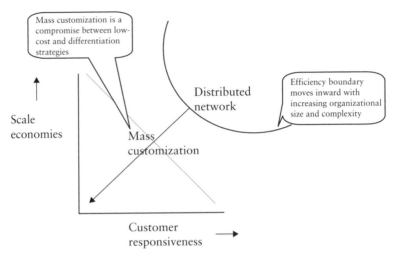

Figure 6.8 Limits of mass customization and distributed network strategies

common platforms – for example, pizza ovens are added to kitchen ranges destined for the Italian market, while fish drawers are added to refrigerators destined for France. A less common intermediate strategy centralizes functions having potential for substantial scale economies, decentralizes functions where responsiveness is critical regardless of cost, and then coordinates across functions using cross-functional teams rather than the organizational hierarchy. There are different terms for this strategy – sometimes it is called a distributed network, sometimes, among global firms, it is called a transnational strategy. Pharmaceutical firms are illustrative. Pharmaceuticals often centralize basic research, decentralize clinical trials of new compounds, centralize bulk manufacturing, decentralize fill-and-finish operations, centralize marketing, decentralize sales, and then delegate coordination to cross-functional teams.

Mass customization and the distributed network/transnational strategy have some limitations, as can be seen in figure 6.8. Mass customization, while conceptually straightforward, is a compromise between low cost and differentiation. It does not avoid the tradeoff between these two polar strategies. Rather, it is located squarely between them. The distributed network/transnational strategy pursues scale economies and customer responsiveness simultaneously but at a price. Network organizations are inherently complicated and difficult to manage (consider again the pharmaceutical example), and coordination costs grow exponentially with the size and complexity of the network. This creates an efficiency boundary beyond which the costs of coordinating the network exceed the benefits of scale economies and customer responsiveness. Indeed, as shown in figure 6.8, this efficiency boundary is concave and moves downward and to the left with organizational size and complexity. Figure 6.8 shows, in other words, that the benefits of the distributed network/transnational strategy are rapidly offset by higher coordination costs as size and complexity increase in distributed networks or transnational firms.

The organizational design implementing ABPA does not suffer the same liabilities. Unlike mass customization, it is not a compromise. Rather, it pursues low cost and differentiation simultaneously by separating the back end from the front end of the firm, and then seeking scale economies at the back end and customer responsiveness at the front end. Unlike the distributed network/transnational strategy, the organizational design implementing ABPA does not require complex coordinating mechanisms. Rather, it assigns distinct missions to front-end and back-end units and supports these missions with fine-grained cost and revenue data: the front end is accountable for customer profitability and for designing products and services that can be sold profitably to customers, while the back end is accountable for delivering products and services at costs and to specifications determined by the front end.

A consequence of this organizational design is a subtle but critical shift in the relationship of generic low-cost and differentiation strategies to each other. Normally, we think of the two strategies as independent and, possibly, antagonistic: the low-cost strategy drives the cost side of the ledger, while differentiation strategy drives revenues. With ABPA, the low-cost and differentiation strategies become complementary: the low-cost strategy aims to minimize costs at the back end given the specifications of products and services supplied by the front end, while the differentiation strategy aims to maximize revenues net of costs at the front end. Figure 6.9 illustrates how ABPA joins the low-cost and differentiation strategies by measuring the costs and revenue consequences of activities and transactions performed for customers. Absent fine-grained cost and revenue data, this connection could not be made. One of the lessons of ABPA, then, is that the customer is the lynchpin connecting the otherwise disparate front-end and back-end strategies.

A general point should not be overlooked. Historically, there has been a close connection between performance measures and firms'

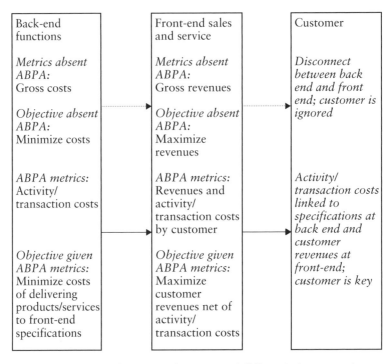

Figure 6.9 How ABPA connects low-cost and differentiation strategies

strategic capabilities. The multiunit firm capable of decentralized operations, for example, did not exist before return-on-asset (ROA) accounting became available. Absent ROA, there was no way to compare the financial performance of business units reliably. Similarly, firms capable of decentralized strategizing and pursuing low-cost and differentiation strategies simultaneously will depend on ABPA-like metrics and organizational designs utilizing these metrics. Absent ABPA-like metrics connecting revenues with costs customer by customer, decentralizing strategizing to customer sales and service units and pursuing the low-cost and differentiation strategies simultaneously would prove extremely challenging.

Balancing centralized and decentralized strategizing

A book subtitled "Beyond the Balanced Scorecard" should return to the notion of balance before closing. As shown in chapter 4, the balanced scorecard is not a particularly effective tool for appraising and compensating people's performance. Two problems are endemic in scorecard-based compensation systems, finding the right scorecard measures, that is scorecard measures driving bottom-line performance, and combining scorecard measures, which are inherently dissimilar, into a single performance appraisal and compensation payout. The complexity of GFS's implementation of the scorecard may have exacerbated these problems, but these problems remain nevertheless. Even the staunchest proponents of scorecard-based measurement systems acknowledge that it is risky to use scorecard measures to evaluate and compensate people.[3]

The same proponents of the balanced scorecard argue that scorecard measures can and should be used to manage strategy, in other words to gauge progress toward strategic objectives. The scorecard, it is argued, helps translate a firm's strategic vision into quantitative measures of success, communicate the vision by setting goals, and learn from experience by comparing results with expectations. This claim is nearly irrefutable: a strategic vision cannot be implemented in any large organization until measures and milestones are put in place, and a strategy cannot be tested until results are compared with expectations. This said, it should be pointed out that using the balanced scorecard to manage a firm's strategy represents a dramatic shift from using the scorecard to measure the performance of people as well as of the firm as a whole. Figure 6.10 illustrates how dramatic this shift is. The rows of figure 6.10 show the four major categories of scorecard measures – financial, customer, internal process, learning and innovation – over time. The columns on which the rows are superimposed represent performance in the four scorecard categories at different points in time, for example quarterly results in these categories. Initially, the value of the scorecard was believed to lie in the columns, in its capacity to capture the performance of the firm in a set of financial and non-financial measures. This objective has proved elusive, and the columns shown in figure 6.10 have largely disappeared from discourse surrounding the scorecard. The rows remain. The rhetoric about transforming strategy into action notwithstanding, the scorecard has become a device for tracking progress toward financial and non-financial targets, which are derived intuitively from the firm's strategy. The connections between scorecard categories and measures and the long-term performance of the firm – its economic performance – remain hypothetical and untested, as they were ten years ago.

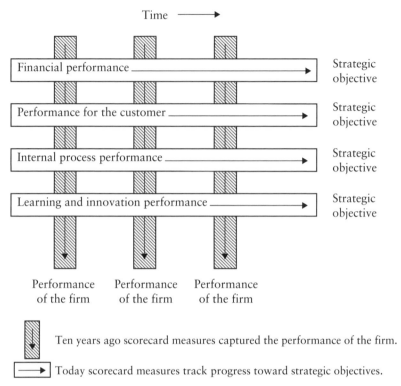

 Ten years ago scorecard measures captured the performance of the firm.

Today scorecard measures track progress toward strategic objectives.

Figure 6.10 The changing significance of the balanced scorecard

There is nothing wrong, in principle, with using the balanced score-card framework to organize the implementation of strategy provided some hidden assumptions are recognized. One hidden assumption is this: the strategy of the firm originates in the vision of senior managers, and choices among strategic alternatives remain the prerogative of senior management. To be sure, overall financial targets, capital allocation, and corporate imperatives – the must-dos of business – will remain senior management prerogatives. Alcoa's corporate objective of an injury-free workplace originated in senior management. This objective was then communicated throughout the organization and reinforced when people who covered up safety breaches lost their jobs. Another hidden assumption is that connections between high-level strategic objectives and specific measures applied at the operating level can somehow be intuited. The strategy maps recommended by proponents of the balanced scorecard help to organize the process of intuiting connections between high-level strategic objectives and operational measures, to be sure, but the connections are derived intuitively nonetheless. Go back to GFS's experience with the balanced scorecard. GFS's senior management chose to weight overall GFS satisfaction heavily because they believed overall satisfaction to be the best predictor of bottom-line results. After-the-fact analysis of GFS's experience proved this intuition erroneous. A twenty-item branch quality index was predictive of the financial performance of GFS's branches. Overall GFS satisfaction contained no information relevant to financial performance. The only virtue of overall GFS satisfaction was that it was convenient because it could be compared across diverse products and markets.

The ABPA approach to performance measurement opens the possibility of decentralizing strategizing to local units. Think again of GFS. GFS offers a large array of products to diverse customer segments worldwide. Ask two questions. First, can any strategic vision originating in senior management and any set of performance measures derived from this vision guide the actions of GFS's people vis-à-vis their customers and competitors globally? The geographic scope of GFS's businesses and the range of GFS's product offerings suggest not. Second, could GFS localize its strategizing by implementing ABPA-like systems that enable managers to identify the drivers of financial performance for *their* customers? A small example from the lore of GFS illustrates the importance of localizing strategies. In Southeast Asia, courtesy and speed are synonymous. In much of Latin American, courtesy is a cup of coffee.

We should be mindful of history. Large US firms began strategizing less than 100 years ago and only after they implemented organizational designs separating strategic from operational responsibilities, the former retained by senior management, the latter delegated to individual business units. This separation became possible once firms learned how to calculate return on investment and, in turn, used ROI to allocate capital to their operating units. The question raised here is whether responsibility for strategizing should be delegated downward as well, with top management retaining responsibility for the overall direction of the business, its financial results, and systems facilitating decentralized strategizing. Decentralized strategizing, like decentralization of operations nearly 100 years ago, will require new performance metrics. The suggestion made in this book is that these new metrics will be fine-grained ABPA-like metrics that enable people to connect their actions directly with the profitability of the firm.

The bottom, bottom line

This chapter explored some issues of managing and strategizing under ABPA. There were several key points:

- Any organizational design for implementing ABPA must specify where in the organization the elements of the performance chain – activities, costs, customers, and revenues – should be joined. For service organizations, I suggested that these elements are best joined in front-end customer sales and service units separated from back-end functional units. The experience of manufacturing firms, by contrast, suggests that the elements of the performance chain are best joined in production units.

- The separation of front-end customer sales and service units from back-end functions allows front-end units to focus on customer profitability and its drivers while back-end units focus on delivering products and services at costs and to specifications determined by front-end units.

- Internet portals extend this organizational design by imposing a market interface between front-end and back-end units. Portals focus relentlessly on customer metrics and assume that the market will supply back-end functions efficiently. Going forward, firms utilizing ABPA-like metrics that join customers with activities and costs will be in direct competition with web-based firms focusing solely on customers.

- ABPA extends the strategic capabilities of firms by allowing them to decentralize much of their strategizing and to pursue low-cost and differentiation strategies simultaneously.

- A balance between centralized and decentralized strategizing is required in complex global firms. Nearly 100 years ago, ROI metrics allowed firms to decentralize their operations. Today, ABPA-like metrics allow firms to decentralize their strategizing.

Notes

Introduction

1. Bill Birchard, "Making it count," *CFO: The Magazine for Senior Financial Executives*, 11, 10 (October 1995): 42.
2. Walid Mougayar, "The new portal math," *Business 2.0*, January 2000: 245.
3. A 1996 Institute of Management Accountants survey asked managers to indicate whether they were undertaking "a major overhaul" of their current measures or replacing their entire performance measurement system. Fully 60 percent said they were. The 2001 IMA survey found that 80 percent of firms had made significant changes in their performance measurement systems in the previous three years, 50 percent were currently making changes, and 33 percent of firms experienced these changes as "a major overhaul."
4. Birchard, "Making it count."
5. John Goff, "Controller burnout," *CFO: The Magazine for Senior Financial Executives*, 11, 9 (September 1995): 60.
6. Institute of Management Accountants, Cost Management Group, *Cost Management Update*, 32 (October 1993), 49 (March 1995), 64 (June 1996), 74 (April 1997), 105 (March 2000), and 115 (March 2001).
7. The major books are Robert Kaplan and David Norton, *The Balanced Scorecard: Translating Strategy into Action* (Boston: Harvard Business School Press, 1996); Kaplan and Norton, *The Strategy-Focused Organization* (Boston: Harvard Business School Press, 2000); Nils-Goran Olve, Jan Roy, and Magnus Wetter, *Performance Drivers: A Practical Guide to Using the Balanced Scorecard* (New York: John Wiley, 1999). The Harvard Business School Publishing website lists 132 books, articles, and cases on the balanced scorecard.
8. Robert Kaplan and David Norton, "The balanced scorecard-measures that drive performance," *Harvard Business Review*, 70, 1 (January–February 1992): 71, 73
9. Many economists cling to this view, relying on Hayek's theorem that prices are "sufficient statistics."

10. Lori Calabro, "On balance: almost 10 years after developing the balanced scorecard, authors Robert Kaplan and David Norton share what they've learned," *CFO: The Magazine for Senior Financial Executives*, 17, 2 (February 2001): 72–78.

11. Robert Kaplan and David Norton, "Transforming the balanced scorecard from performance measurement to strategic management: part I," *Accounting Horizons*, 15, 1 (March 2001): 87–104. Kaplan and Norton criticize academic research for not grasping the importance of the scorecard as a management system.

12. The full list of 117 measures is currently used by Skandia, the Swedish financial services firm. See Leif Edvinsson and Michael S. Malone, *Intellectual Capital: Realizing Your Company's True Value by Finding Its Hidden Brainpower* (New York: HarperBusiness, 1997).

13. Franklin M. Fisher, "Accounting data and the economic performance of firms," *Journal of Accounting and Public Policy*, 7 (1988): 253–260.

14. It does not matter whether these cash flows are retained by the firm or distributed to shareholders as dividends – all that matters is that cash flows are used efficiently.

15. The loss of critical performance information was one of the key reasons functional organizational designs were replaced by divisional designs from the 1920s through the 1960s.

16. The value chain is illustrated in Michael Porter and Victor E. Millar, "How information gives you competitive advantage." *Harvard Business Review*, 63, 4 (July–August 1985): 149–160.

17. See Marshall Meyer, "What happened to middle management?" in Ivar Berg and Arne L. Kalleberg (eds.), *Sourcebook of Labor Markets* (New York: Kluwer Academic/Plenum, 2001), ch. 18.

1 Why are performance measures so bad?

1. *Oxford English Dictionary*, 2nd edn. (Oxford: Oxford University Press, 1989), "P," p. 689 (emphasis added).

2. Shakespeare, in *Macbeth*, captures the difference between expected and actual performance in a different context. Macduff asks, "What three things does drink especially provoke?" The porter replies, in part, "...Lechery, sir, it provokes and unprovokes; it provokes the desire, but takes away the performance" (act II, scene iii).

3. Franklin M. Fisher, "Accounting data and the economic performance of the firm," *Journal of Accounting and Public Policy*, 7 (1988): 256.

4. US firms often solicit employee contributions to agencies like the United Way, an association of community-based charitable

organizations. Each firm sets a target for total contributions, and progress toward this target is displayed on a stylized thermometer, as in figure 1.3.

5. Todd Buchholz quotes Paul Samuelson as saying that "most portfolio managers should go out of business – take up plumbing, teach Greek..." See *New Ideas from Dead Economists*, rev. edn. (New York: Penguin, 1990), p. 278 and p. 322, footnote 1.

6. Eugene F. Fama, "Random walks in stock market prices," *Financial Analysts Journal*, 51 (1995): 75–81.

7. There is great variety in the performance measures used by entrepreneurial firms. See Gregory B. Murphy, Jeff W. Trailer, and Robert C. Hill, "Measuring performance in entrepreneurship research," *Journal of Business Research*, 36 (1996), pp. 15–23.

8. There are also substantial lags between functioning and financial results – sometimes the lags are infinite since financial results never materialize – in firms whose core technology is unproven, biotech and internet firms in particular.

9. Simon Hussain, "Lead indicator models and UK analysts' earnings forecasts," *Accounting and Business Research*, 28 (1998): 271–280.

10. Mehdi Sheikholeslami, Michael D. Wilson, and J. Roger Selin, "The impact of CEO turnover on security analysts' forecast accuracy," *Journal of Applied Business Research*, 14 (1998): 71–75.

11. Michael Useem, *Executive Defense* (Cambridge, MA: Harvard University Press, 1976), p. 76.

12. See Charles Fombrun and Mark Shanley, "What's in a name? Reputation building and corporate strategy," *Academy of Management Journal*, 33 (1990): 233–258. The impact of a firm's reputation on its subsequent performance is the firm-level counterpart of the "Matthew effect" in science.

13. If the firm consists of identical business units performing the same functions (for example chain stores and franchise restaurants), then non-financial measures will roll up from business units to the firm as a whole and cascade down from the firm to business units.

14. Richard J. Dowen and W. Scott Bauman, "Financial statements, investment analyst forecasts and abnormal returns," *Journal of Business Finance and Accounting*, 22 (1995): 431–449.

15. James J. Cordeiro and D. Donald Kent, Jr., "Do EVA(TM) adopters outperform their industry peers? Evidence from security analyst earnings forecasts," *American Business Review*, 19 (2001): 57–63.

16. Roger J. Best and Ronald W. Best, "Earnings expectations and the relative information content of dividend and earnings announcements," *Journal of Economics and Finance*: 24 (2000): 232–245; Michael

J. Gombola and Feng-Ying Liu, "The signaling power of specially designated dividends," *Journal of Financial and Quantitative Analysis*, 34 (1999): 409–424.

17. William R. Baber, Jong-Dae Kim, and Krishna R. Kumar, "On the use of intra-industry information to improve earnings forecasts," *Journal of Business Finance and Accounting*, 26 (1999): 1177–1198.

18. Jonathan Low and Tony Siesfeld, "Measures that matter: Wall Street considers non-financial performance more than you think," *Strategy and Leadership*, 26 (1998): 24–30.

19. Oliver E. Williamson, *Markets and Hierarchies: Analysis and Antitrust Implications* (New York: Free Press, 1975), p. 150 (emphasis in original).

20. Louis V. Gerstner, Jr., and M. Helen Anderson, "The chief financial officer as activist," *Harvard Business Review*, 54, 5 (September–October 1976): 100.

21. Joel M. Stern, "One way to build value in your firm," Financial Executive, 6, 6 (November 1990), p. 51. See also G. Bennett Stewart, *The Quest For Value* (New York: Harper Business, 1991).

22. "The real key to creating wealth," *Fortune*, 128, 6 (September 20, 1993): 38–44.

23. Maggie Topkis, "A new way to find bargains," *Fortune*, 134, 11 (December 9, 1996): 265.

24. Gary C. Biddle, Robert M. Bowen, and James S. Wallace, "Evidence on the relative and incremental information content of EVA, residual income, earnings and operating cash flow," unpublished manuscript, Washington University (1996).

25. James L. Dodd and Shimin Chen, "EVA: a new panacea?" *Business and Economic Review*, 42, 4 (July–September, 1996): 26–28. Dodd and Chen also suggest that when calculating EVA it is inefficient to make the adjustments in earnings suggested by Stern, Stewart.

26. Kaplan and Norton had no particular theory of the scorecard and still do not. See Robert S. Kaplan, "Innovation action research: creating new management theory and practice," *Journal of Management Accounting Research*, 10 (1998): 89–118.

27. Robert Eccles and Nitin Nohira, *Beyond the Hype* (Boston, Harvard Business School Press, 1992), pp. 159–163.

28. The Sears business model is reported in Anthony J. Rucci, Steven P. Kirn, and Richard T. Quinn, "The employee-customer profit chain at Sears," *Harvard Business Review*, 76, 1 (January–February 1998): 82–97.

29. Sears' customer satisfaction measures are not indicated in the Rucci et al. article.

30. The characterizations of measures and outcomes in figures 1.6 and 1.7 are drawn from several sources, most importantly Carolyn Brancatom, *New Corporate Performance Measures* (New York: The Conference Board, 1995), several reports of the Royal Society for the encouragement of the Arts, Manufactures & Commerce on "Tomorrow's company," and personal correspondence with John E. Balkcom, a Sibson & Co. consultant.

31. MVA, like EVA, is a trademark of Stern, Stewart & Co.

32. George Johnson, *Fire in the Mind* (New York: Knopf, 1995), p. 177.

33. Personal communication with John Balkcom.

2 The running down of performance measures

1. See Stephen Jay Gould, "Trends as change in variance: a new slant on progress and directionality in evolution," *Journal of Paleontology*, 62 (1988): 319–329. See also Gould, *Full House: The Spread of Excellence from Plato to Darwin* (New York: Harmony House, 1996).

2. Gould, "Trends as change in variance," p. 326.

3. Gould, *Full House*, p. 119.

4. See John Thorn and Peter Palmer, *Total Baseball*, 2nd edn. (New York: Warner, 1991), pp. 682–692.

5. Murray Chass, "The best buys in baseball," *New York Times*, March 4, 1992, pp. C1 and C4) compared underpaid (average salary $110,000) with overpaid (average salary $3.5 million) baseball players and found that their batting averages differed by only .005.

6. Alfred A. Marcus, Mary L. Nichols, and Gregory E. McAvoy, "The managerial determinants of nuclear power safety," Strategic Management Research Center, University of Minnesota, March 1993.

7. Graphs for significant events, safety system failures, and radiation exposure are omitted for purposes of brevity. The pattern for all five safety measures is similar. Gould's observation about evolutionary change bears repeating as it applies with some force in this instance: the overall improvement in mean safety outcomes is due to decreased variance across plants.

8. Mark Rechtin, "As quality gap narrows, Power rethinks the IQS," *Automotive News*, May 12, 1997, p. 3.

9. Paul DiMaggio and Walter W. Powell, "The iron cage revisited: institutional isomorphism and collective rationality in organizational fields," *American Sociological Review*, 48 (1983): 147–160.

10. Duncan Neuhauser, "The relationship between administrative activities and hospital performance: an empirical study," University of Chicago, 1971, p. 17.

11. Mark Rechtin, "As quality gap narrows," p. 28.
12. Personal communication with Alfred A. Marcus, University of Minnesota.
13. "The test under stress," *New York Times Magazine*, January 10, 1999.
14. Alfred J. Reiss, *The Police and the Public* (New Haven: Yale University Press, 1971).
15. Peter M. Blau, *The Dynamics of Bureaucracy*, 2nd edn. (Chicago: University of Chicago Press, 1963), pp. 37–38, 45–46.
16. Patrick Healy, "Ahead of the curve: some professors battling against grade inflation," *Boston Globe*, February 7, 2001, p. A1.
17. Richard Rothstein, "Doubling of A's at Harvard: grade inflation or brains?" *New York Times*, December 5, 2001, p. D8.
18. James L. Medoff and Katerine G. Abraham, "Experience, performance, and earnings," *Quarterly Journal of Economics*, 95 (1980): 703–736.
19. Sylvester E. Berki, *Hospital Economics* (Lexington: Lexington Books, 1972); David B. Smith and Arnold D. Kaluzny, *The White Labyrinth: A Guide to the Health Care System* (Ann Arbor: Health Administration Press, 1986).
20. Dana Priest, "Pennsylvania rates hospitals, surgeons on heart bypass patient deaths," *Washington Post*, November 20, 1992, p. A3.
21. Joseph Berger, "Fernandez seeks to end test ranking," *New York Times*, June 9, 1992, p. B3.
22. These data were generously supplied by David Mauer, who has published extensively from them.
23. Glenn R. Carroll and Michael T. Hannan, *The Demography of Corporations and Industries* (Princeton: Princeton University Press, 1999), ch. 13.
24. This account of the "Measurements Project" is taken from Ronald G. Greenwood, *Managerial Decentralization; A Study of the General Electric Philosophy* (Lexington: Lexington Books, 1974).
25. J. Holusha, "A call for kinder managers at GE," *New York Times*, March 4, 1992, pp. D1 and D6.
26. William M. Carley, "To keep GE's profits rising, Welch pushes quality-control program," *Wall Street Journal*, January 13, 1997, pp. A1 and A8.
27. The SPI4 database is described in *The PIMS Competitive Strategy DataBase* (Cambridge, MA: Strategic Planning Institute, 1988).
28. These correlations are shown in the appendix to this chapter.
29. Control variables are utilized and tests of statistical significance for differences between blocks of correlations are shown in Marshall Meyer, "Organizational design and the performance paradox," in Richard

Swedberg (ed.), *Explorations in Economic Sociology* (New York: Russell Sage Foundation, 1993), ch. 10.

30. Harrison C. White, *Identity and Control: A Structural Theory of Social Action* (Princeton: Princeton University Press, 1992).

3 In search of balance

1. Robert Kaplan and David Norton, *The Balanced Scorecard* (Boston: Harvard Business School Press, 1996), p. 2.

2. The most heavily weighted item in the branch quality index (45%) asked customers to rate "the overall quality of [the branch's] service against your expectations" on a five-point scale The other items include the quality of tellers versus expectations (7.5%), six additional items concerning tellers (7.5%), quality of other branch personnel versus expectations (7.5%), six additional items concerning non-teller employees (7.5%), quality of automated teller machines (ATMs) versus expectations (7.5%), three additional items concerning ATMs (7.5%), and one item measuring problem incidence (10%). The branch quality index was considered superior because multiple-item measures reduce measurement error. This is the case, however, only if the resulting construct is unidimensional (i.e. all of the questions measure the same construct).

3. A household is a family or business-unit group that makes joint banking decisions. Tier I households have total combined balances (including investment balances) in excess of $100,000; tier II households have balances in excess of $10,000. Footings are consumer and business/professional liabilities plus consumer and business/professional assets (excluding mortgages).

4. Premier households had balances in excess of $100,000 and maintained investment portfolios at GFS.

5. Performance management was defined as a manager's ability to "achieve goals by coaching, motivating, empowering, hiring, supporting, promoting, recognizing, and challenging staff." Although employee satisfaction was considered in evaluating the people category, employee satisfaction surveys were not conducted on a regular basis, making the quarterly assessment of this measure qualitative. Moreover, there was no statistically significant correlation between the employee satisfaction scores from a 1996 survey and the subjective "people" scores given by area directors in the first and second quarters of 1996, indicating that quantitative employee satisfaction measures received little weight in evaluating managerial performance on this dimension.

6. Formal goals were not provided for the control, people, and standards categories, but an audit rating of "3" or lower is "below par" performance in the control category.

7. The branch manager, however, could exercise discretion in allocating the bonus pool among branch employees. Thus, if a branch met all of its targets under the 1993 PIP, the branch manager received a quarterly bonus of 15 percent of base salary, the bonus pool for branch employees was 7.5 percent of base salaries, but bonuses for individual branch employees varied at the discretion of the branch manager.

8. GFS's scorecard consisted of thirty-seven measures in six scorecard categories. By contrast, the scorecards of Metro Bank and National Insurance that are discussed by Kaplan and Norton (*The Balanced Scorecard*, pp. 155, 157) had twenty and twenty-one measures respectively, both in four scorecard categories.

9. A 1 percent increase in branch quality caused a subsequent 0.04 percent increase in revenues and 0.22 percent increase in margins.

10. A 1 percent increase in branch quality caused a subsequent 0.2 percent increase in retail households and 0.3 percent increase in business/professional households.

11. This analysis was restricted to four quarters, the third quarter of 1995 through the second quarter of 1996, for which item-by-item data were available. The component items in the branch-quality index were not reported on branch-manager scorecards.

12. A 1 percent increase in teller quality caused a subsequent 0.4 percent increase in revenues and 0.5 percent increase in margins.

13. This is consistent with the experience of branch managers who believe that satisfaction among retail customers surveyed by GFS declines as attention is diverted to the smaller but more profitable segment of business/professional and premier customers not included in customer surveys.

14. Kaplan and Norton, *The Balanced Scorecard*, p. 218.

15. GFS's cost of funds is a complex and proprietary calculation that takes into account prevailing interest rates, interest paid on liability balances, and other factors.

16. GFS, like other retail banks, believes that cross-selling can generate ongoing fee revenues from current deposit and loan customers. Part of GFS's sales-focused strategy is a personal financial planning tool intended to increase customers' awareness of insurance and investment products.

17. A consumer household consists of one or more related people maintaining one or more GFS accounts.

18. Some of these acquisitions of consumer money market checking accounts may be due to conversion of existing ordinary checking accounts into money market accounts. An acquisition of a consumer money market checking account is recorded – and a sale is credited to a customer relationship manager – when an ordinary checking account is converted to a money market checking account.

4 From cost drivers to revenue drivers

1. The parts of an airline journey most easily reduced to specifications, notably schedules, safety, and prices, are comparable for most airlines. Airlines thus compete on customer service, which cannot be reduced to simple specifications.
2. See, for example, Hau L. Lee, V. Padmanabhan, and Seungjin Whang, "The bullwhip effect in supply chains," *Sloan Management Review*, 38, 3 (Spring 1998): 93–102.
3. Customer-initiated and customer-support transactions are distinguished because transactions beginning at the same point in the organization may flow through different channels depending on the customer and product.
4. Indirect activities consist of management, supervision, and administration incidental to the transaction.
5. Short-term variable costs are direct labor and costs. Long-term variable costs are costs of supervision and administration incurred by indirect activities. Capacity costs are costs of equipment and premises. Fixed costs insensitive to the volume of transactions are omitted in calculating activity costs.
6. Customer net revenue (CNR) is the sum of fees charged to the customer and net revenues earned on balances. Net revenues are balances times spreads, that is, gross revenues less the cost of funds.
7. Variable costs accounted for about 28 percent of total costs initially.
8. Robert S. Kaplan and Robin Cooper, *Cost and Effect* (Boston: Harvard Business School Press, 1998), pp. 183–197.
9. Overall satisfaction with GFS as a place to do business, measured as the percentage of customers falling in the top two categories of a five-point scale, increased from 71 percent in June 1992 to 95 percent in December 1993. Overall customer satisfaction, measured on a five-point scale, remained at or above 90 percent thereafter. The percentage of customers willing to recommend GFS increased from 72 to 97 percent in the same period.
10. Forty-two percent of customers surveyed in June 1992 reported problems, while only 8 percent reported problems in December 1994.

Inquiries and investigations resulting from customer complaints, moreover, fell from 7.8 to 1.6 per thousand accounts from December 1992 to December 1994.

11. This correlation is not statistically significant due to the small number of cases.

12. Kaplan and Cooper, *Cost and Effect*, ch. 10; also Harvard Business School case study "Kanthall" (9–190–002).

13. Fixed costs insensitive to the volume of transactions (e.g. financial control costs) were ignored in calculating activity costs.

14. Marshall W. Meyer, "Productivity cultures and competition in the global marketplace: cases from Hong Kong," in J. T. Li, Anne S. Tsui, and Elizabeth Weldon (eds.), *Management and Organizations in Chinese Context* (New York: St. Martin's Press, 2000), ch. 12.

15. In the USA, GFS customer-satisfaction surveys sampled twenty-five customers per branch per month through the end of 1999. This number was reduced substantially beginning in 2000.

16. Peter J. Kolesar, "Vision, values, milestones: Paul O'Neill starts total quality at Alcoa,"*California Management Review*, 35, 3 (Spring 1993): 133–165.

17. Michael Lewis, "O'Neill's list," *New York Times Magazine*, January 13, 2002, p. 24.

18. Jennifer J. Laabs, "Alcoa unit president forced to resign after failing to report safety violations," *Personnel Journal*, 75, 9 (September 1996): 12.

19. Philip Selznick, *Leadership in Administration* (Berkeley: University of California Press, 1957).

5 Learning from ABPA

1. Recall from chapter 1 the deficiencies of aggregate (or coarse-grained) measures, non-financial measures especially.

2. David Kreps, *A Course on Microeconomic Theory* (Princeton: Princeton University Press, 1990), pp. 611–612.

3. Steven Spear and H. Kent Bowen, "Decoding the DNA of the Toyota production system," *Harvard Business Review*, 77, 5 (September–October, 1999): 99.

4. Paul S. Adler and Robert E. Cole, "Designed for learning: a tale of two auto plants," *Sloan Management Review*, 34, 3 (spring 1993): 90.

5. John Paul MacDuffie, "The road to 'root cause': shop-floor problem-solving at three auto assembly plants," *Management Science*, 43 (1997): 479–502.

6. CMM is registered in the US Patent and Trademark Office.

7. The five include the initial stage, where success depends on leadership and heroics; the repeatable stage, where basic management processes (scheduling, budgeting, measurement functionality) are in place; the defined stage, where the software development process is documented and standardized; the managed stage, where detailed measures are collected and the development process is quantified throughout; and the optimizing stage, where continuous feedback from measurement is used to improve the software development process.

8. Some KPAs include software quality assurance at the repeatable stage; integrated software management at the defined stage; quantitative process management at the managed stage; and process change management at the optimizing stage.

9. The most recent report, "Process maturity profile of the software community: 1999 year end update," was released in March 2000.

10. P. K. Lawlis, R. M. Flowe, and J. B. Thorndahl, "A correlational study of the CMM and software development performance," *CrossTalk: The Journal of Defensive Engineering*, 8, 9 (September, 1995): 21–25.

11. M. S. Krishnan, "Cost and quality considerations in software product management," doctoral dissertation, School of Industrial Administration, Carnegie Mellon University, 1996.

12. James Herbsleb, David Zubrow, Denis Goldenson, Will Hayes, and Mark Paulk, "Software quality and the capability maturity model," *Communications of the Association for Computer Machinery*, 40, 6 (June, 1997): 30–40.

13. Figure 5.2 is based on estimates made by the GFS Country A retail business in 1993–94 (see chapter 4).

14. Financial measures are usually dropped from scorecards cascaded below the level of business units.

6 Managing and strategizing with ABPA

1. See James D. Thompson, *Organizations in Action* (New York: McGraw-Hill, 1967).

2. Don Tapscott, David Ticoll, and Alex Lowy, *Digital Capital: Harnessing the Power of Business Webs* (Boston: Harvard Business School Press, 2000). Quoted from "Relationships rule," *Business 2.0*, May 2000.

3. Robert S. Kaplan and David P. Norton, "Using the balanced scorecard as a strategic management system," *Harvard Business Review*, 74, 1 (January–February 1996): 81.

Index